GONGORA'S POETIC
TEXTUAL TRADITION

DIANE CHAFFEE-SORACE

GONGORA'S POETIC TEXTUAL TRADITION

An analysis of selected variants,
versions and imitations
of his shorter poems

TAMESIS BOOKS LIMITED
LONDON

Colección Támesis
SERIE A - MONOGRAFIAS, CXXXII

DISTRIBUTORS:

Spain:
  Editorial Castalia,
  Zurbano, 39,
  28010 Madrid

United States and Canada:
  Longwood Publishing Group,
  27 South Main Street,
  Wolfeboro, New Hampshire 03894-2069, U.S.A.

Great Britain and rest of the world:
  Grant and Cutler Ltd.,
  55-57 Great Marlborough Street,
  London W1V 2AY

Depósito legal: M. 35084-1988

Printed in Spain by Talleres Gráficos de SELECCIONES GRÁFICAS
Carretera de Irún, km. 11,500 - 28049 Madrid

for
TAMESIS BOOKS LIMITED
LONDON

TABLE OF CONTENTS

For Jim

PREFACE

This book originated from research on the sixteenth and seventeenth centuries carried out at Duke University, specifically work partially relating to my doctoral thesis, which was also devoted to the poetry of Luis de Góngora. To Professor Bruce W. Wardropper I owe the initial stimulus for my interest in Góngora studies. I am especially grateful, in addition, to Professor Mary Lee Cozad for her perceptive reading of my manuscript and for her most important suggestions and criticism. My thanks extend to Professor Louise O. Vasvari and again to Professor Wardropper, who read a section of Chapter II in its final stages as an article entitled «The Endings of Góngora's 'Servía en Orán al rey'» now published in the BHS, 59, No. 1 (1982), 15-20. I am likewise indebted to Professor Javier S. Herrero and Professor David T. Gies who read a section of Chapter III in its early form, which has since been expanded and published in the RJ with the title «The Elephant and the Rhinoceros: Stages of a Góngora Sonnet», 34 (1983), 308-17. This article grew out of my talk, «The Elephant and the Rhinoceros: A First Look at an Earlier Source of a Gongorine Sonnet», read at the Louisiana Conference on Hispanic Languages and Literatures in 1982 and published in the selected proceedings of that meeting. My articles from the BHS and RJ appear here by kind permission. I am very appreciative of Professor Marta E. Altisent and Professor Samuel G. Armistead for their valuable suggestions concerning my translations of the three Góngora poems «Vn buhonero ha empleado», «Trepan los Gitanos», and «Hermana Marica». I also wish to thank the editorial board of RomN for allowing me to reprint my paper «The Poetic Artistry of Góngora's 'No son todos ruiseñores': To End or Not to End», 22, No. 1 (1981-82), 74-77, in slightly altered form in Chapter II, the board of the RF for permission to incorporate my article «Imitation as the Explanation for Chronology: Two Versions of a Gongorine Text», 93, No. 3/4 (1981), 383-86, into Chapter III, and the editors of the SMCLL for consenting to the use in Chapter III of information from my essay «Góngora's 'Mientras por competir con tu cabello': Further Thoughts on Imitation and Chronology» (forthcoming in 1988).

The Hispanic Society of America has graciously permitted me to reproduce in my book nine short poems from Góngora's Obras poéticas,

ed. Raymond Foulché-Delbosc (1921; New York: The Hispanic Society of America, 1970). The University of California Press has authorized me to include the sonnet «Grandes mas q̃ elefantes y Abbadas» from Arthur Lee-Francis Askins's edition of the Cancioneiro de corte e de magnates, *University of California Publications in Modern Philology, No. 84 (Berkeley: University of California Press, 1968). The Consejo Superior de Investigaciones Científicas has allowed me to reproduce Garcilaso de la Vega's sonnet «En tanto que de rosa i açucena» from his* Obras con anotaciones de Fernando de Herrera *(Sevilla: Alonso de la Barrera, 1580), facs. ed. Antonio Gallego Morell (Madrid: CSIC, 1973) and the two anonymous poems «Hermano Perico» and «Hermana Juanilla» from the* Romancero general 1600, 1604, 1605, *ed. Ángel González Palencia, Clásicos Españoles, III-IV (Madrid: CSIC, 1947). The Special Collections Department of the University of Southern California's Edward L. Doheny Library in Los Angeles has kindly lent me the rare book* Varias descripciònes del tiempo, y de las estaciones del año, *compiled by Josef de Valdivieso (Palma: Felipe Guasp, 1817), from which I have copied the sonnet «Mientras que refulgente tu cabello», printed under Góngora's name, for inclusion in Chapter III.*

Finally, no account of my gratitude would be complete without mention of the Dean of Loyola College, who has graciously made possible the publication of this book, my parents, who have generously supported my education, and my husband, who has patiently and lovingly encouraged my efforts.

D. C.-S.

Baltimore, Maryland.

ABBREVIATIONS

AAL	Academia Argentina de Letras
BAE	Biblioteca de Autores Españoles
BHS	*Bulletin of Hispanic Studies*
CSIC	Consejo Superior de Investigaciones Científicas
DAI	*Dissertation Abstracts International*
HR	*Hispanic Review*
HSA	Hispanic Society of America
HSMS	Hispanic Seminary of Medieval Studies
IEIIAUB	Institut d'Études Ibériques et Ibéro-Américaines de l'Université de Bordeaux
IEM	Instituto de Estudios Madrileños
MLN	*Modern Language Notes*
RAE	Real Academia Española
RF	*Romanische Forschungen*
RFE	*Revista de Filología Española*
RHi	*Revue Hispanique*
RHL	*Revue d'Histoire Littéraire de la France*
RJ	*Romanistisches Jahrbuch*
RO	*Revista de Occidente*
RomN	*Romance Notes*
RR	*Romanic Review*
SMCLL	*Studies in Modern and Classical Languages and Literatures*
SP	*Studies in Philology*

I

AN INTRODUCTION TO GÓNGORA'S POETIC TEXTUAL TRADITION

Many variants, versions, and imitations characterize Spanish Golden Age poetry. Whereas Garcilaso's famous sonnet «En tanto que de rosa y azucena» has one noted variant line, renowned texts such as Luis de Góngora's «La más bella niña», Francisco de Quevedo's «Miré los muros de la patria mía», and Fray Luis de León's «Rojo sol, que con llama gloriosa» exist in two or even three versions, each with several lines or strophes different from the other versions. Góngora and poets who were his contemporaries revised much of their own verse in addition to imitating the work of their predecessors. An analysis of Góngora's poetry, which in particular suffered many alterations, sheds light on the major textual problems that plague much of the study of Spanish Golden Age poetry and elucidates the effects these problems have on both his poetic tradition and that of other poets of his day.

During Góngora's lifetime, a vast amount of his poetry circulated in manuscript, sometimes with his authorization and sometimes without it. The poet's friends and admirers created large numbers of variants by copying and recopying poems that Góngora had sent to them. Moreover, by modifying texts to avoid public censure and censorship, Góngora or his copyists contributed even more variants to his already massive output. Although some of his poems were published during his lifetime, many were collected posthumously for inclusion in *cancioneros* and *romanceros*. Antonio Rodríguez Moñino believed that a special workshop in Córdoba or Madrid existed for the sole purpose of reproducing the poet's works; several such unauthorized volumes of his poetry are in existence today. These collections, some of which have identical titles, include mostly the same poems, and the pages of many volumes correspond almost exactly.[1]

---

[1] ANTONIO RODRÍGUEZ-MOÑINO, *Construcción crítica y realidad histórica en la poesía española de los siglos XVI y XVII* (Madrid: Castalia, 1968), p. 34: «Existen hoy numerosos volúmenes, aproximadamente con el mismo contenido, algunos de ellos con idéntico título, todos extensos, que demuestran el enorme interés que hubo por leer y poseer su obra. Todos estos manuscritos son posteriores a las *Soledades* y al

1

By participating in copying Góngora's poems from circulars or manuscripts that were not always accurate, seventeenth-century anthologists perpetuated variants, some of which were extensive. Juan López de Vicuña supports this contention in his edition of Góngora's poetry, *Obras en verso del Homero español* (1627), when he addresses the reader regarding a few of the problems encountered in collecting the master's poems:

Al Letor[2]

Veinte años ha que comencè a recoger las obras de nuestro Poeta, primero en el mundo. Nunca guardò original della: cuidado costò harto hallarlas, y comunicarselas, que de nueuo las trabajaua: pues quando las poniamos en sus manos, apenas las conocia: tales llegauā despues de auer corrido por muchas copias. Archiuo fue dellas la libreria de don Pedro de Cordoua y Angulo,[3] Cauallero de la Orden de Santiago, Ventiquatro, y natural de Cordoua. De alli han salido algunos traslados. Muchos versos se echaràn menos, algunos que la modestia del Autor no permitiò andar en publico.[4]

Poetic discrepancies of little importance (which include word substitution or deviations in verses or verse order) may have been deliberate changes or mere copying errors. Some variants, however, are of greater significance; they include stanzas added to or subtracted from the authentic texts that Góngora's friend don Antonio Chacón Ponce de León compiled before 1620 with the assistance of the author. These variants may be attributed to censorship in the case of some scatological verses or to the poet's desire to perfect his work in the case of other poems. Góngora's meticulous artistry rarely allowed him to be satisfied with anything he had written, and, on occasion, his rewriting produced variant versions.

In spite of Vicuña's statement that seventeenth-century anthologists perpetuated the variants in Góngora's poetry and Raymond Foulché-Delbosc's affirmation that, for the most part, Góngora did not return to a poem or save the manuscript copy of it once it was written,[5] proof that the poet

---

Polifemo, puesto que incluyen tales obras. Las copias suelen estar hechas con letra clara, buenos márgenes, y no contienen indicaciones críticas o eruditas. Hay, además, códices de otro tipo, pero me parece muy importante señalar la posible existencia en Madrid o en Córdoba de un taller especializado en copiar textos de don Luis. Algunos tomos se corresponden casi a plana y renglón.»

[2] DÁMASO ALONSO, Introduction to *Obras en verso del Homero español* (Madrid: Imprenta del Reino), facs. (Madrid: CSIC, 1963), pp. xxi-xxiii, includes the note that in the HSA there are two copies of the Vicuña edition. One is the original and the other has been altered by Vicuña to avoid censorship and to correct an occasional editorial error.

[3] «Pedro de Córdoua y Angulo» is a mistake for «Pedro de Cárdenas y Angulo», which was corrected in the more innocuous second text.

[4] Vicuña, no pagination (but p. xciii in the facs.).

[5] LUIS DE GÓNGORA, *Obras poéticas,* ed. Raymond Foulché-Delbosc (1921; rpt. New York: HSA, 1970), I, xiii: «Si es cierto que retocó [Góngora] algunas composiciones, es evidente que, en la mayoría de los casos, una vez hecha la poesía, no volvía a

rewrote and modified his work can be found in the following anecdote from Pellicer's *Escrutinio*:

> [Góngora] daba orejas a las advertencias, o censuras, modesto, i con gùsto. Emendaba si avia que, sin presumir: tanto, que haciendo una Nenia a la translacion de los huessos de el insigne Castellano Garci Laso de la Vega a nuevo i mas sumptuoso sepulchro por sus descendientes, una de sus Coplas communicò, i el que la oiò respondiò con el silencio. Preguntòle don Luis: «Que? No es buena?» Replicòsele: «Si, pero no para de Don Luis.» Sintiòlo, con decirle: «Fuerte cosa, que no basten quarenta años de approbacion, para que se me fie?» No se hablò mas en la materia. La noche de este dia se volvieron a veer los dos: i lo primero que Don Luis dixo, fue: «A, señor. Soi como el gato de algalia, que a açotes da el olor. Ia està differente la Copla.» I assi fue, porque se excediò a ssi mismo en ella. (*apud* FOULCHÉ-DELBOSC, I, xiii)

Because no complete edition of Góngora's poetry was published during his lifetime, it was natural that diverse versions and a host of variants were printed in the anthologies of his verse made public after his death. The Vicuña collection of his poetry and an edition by don Gonzalo de Hoces y Córdoba[6] —both accessible to readers for three centuries following the poet's death— were often used as sources by compilers of subsequent anthologies. As with any other unauthorized text, the reliability of these variants is questionable. Alfonso Reyes remarks on the validity of all early editions of Góngora's poetry, but his comment is also applicable to the texts of many Golden Age poets:

> Por una parte, los textos auténticos aparecen corrompidos, incompletos o zurcidos de mano ajena; por otra, le han prohijado al poeta obras extrañas, desposeyéndole en cambio de algunas propias.[7]

Before and after his death in 1627, Góngora's poems were in disarray; some existed in more than one version and the variants were numerous. Fortunately, near the end of his lifetime, Góngora had collaborated with Chacón in compiling a calf-bound *de luxe* manuscript anthology of his poetic works for presentation to the Conde-Duque de Olivares. This anthology was completed and given the poet's authorization by 1620.[8] Because Góngora assisted Chacón, because he did so towards the end of his life and of his career as a poet, and because he did so at the behest of such

---

acordarse de ella, y ni siquiera conservaba el manuscrito o la copia.» The Foulché-Delbosc edition is a diplomatic text of the Chacón manuscript.

[6] *Todas las obras de don Luis de Góngora en varios poemas* (Madrid: Imprenta Real, 1633).

[7] *Cuestiones gongorinas* (Madrid: Espasa-Calpe, 1927), p. 53.

[8] REYES, p. 41. Although the manuscript was «published» in 1628 (i.e. presented to Olivares), its compilation was finished in 1620. This collection is considered by scholars to be the authorized edition of Góngora's poetry because of Góngora's personal participation.

a powerful magnate, this collection of Góngora's works is considered the only authorized contemporary edition. From the poet's point of view, the Chacón texts of his poems represented an improvement over all other versions of which he was aware. Foulché-Delbosc maintains that:

> ... puesto que algunas veces [Góngora] corregía o refundía, no es imposible que dos textos distintos de una misma composición sean igualmente auténticos Pero tampoco es imposible (y este caso es sin duda el más frecuente) que, entre dos textos diferentes, sólo uno —el que consta en el manuscrito Chacón— sea el auténtico, no siendo el otro más que una transcripción defectuosa o adulterada, y, por consecuencia, de valor nulo. (I, xiii-xiv)

Each text in the Chacón manuscript was selected by Góngora from a variety of manuscripts or printed versions assembled by Chacón or supplied by the poet himself. Among the available variants and versions, Góngora chose those that at this late date in his poetic career seemed to him best to represent his mature craft. A sentence from Chacón's dedication to the Conde-Duque de Olivares confirms these assumptions:

> Quando junté todas las [poesías] que la diligencia de don Luis i la mía pudo adquirir en ocho años; quando trabajé con él las emendasse en mi presencia con diferente atención que solía otras vezes, i quando le pedí me informasse de los casos particulares de algunas cuia inteligencia depende de su noticia, me dixesse los sujetos de todas i los años en que hizo cada vna, sólo tuve por fin el interés que mi affic ión a estas obras lograua. (REYES, p. 40)

In spite of the poet's intervention, Chacón's manuscript is not without its flaws. After forty years of writing poetry (1580-1620), the elderly poet, when asked to pick out the best wording from a selection of variants of a given poem and to supply the date of the poem's composition probably would not always have been able to recall what he had originally written or when he had written it.[9] In addition, it is sometimes impossible to determine whether a variant was created by Góngora or whether it was a change made by a censor, a careless copyist, or a creative anthologist. Therefore, the question of authorship or authenticity plays an important role in investigating Góngora's variants and versions, the most significant of which include apocryphal, divergent, and missing endings, confused strophic order, close imitations, and alternate genuine or spurious texts of some of the definitive Góngora poems. An analysis, however, makes it possible to determine the literary effects of a number of variants and versions, some of which are accepted as his by modern critics or proposed

---

[9] MIGUEL ARTIGAS, *Don Luis de Góngora y Argote* (Madrid: RAE, 1925), p. 214, cites evidence of defects in the Chacón manuscript as noted throughout Foulché-Delbosc's edition of Góngora's poetry: «En un tercer tomo reúne el señor Foulché las poesías —algunas nada satíricas— que seguramente son de Góngora, y que, no obstante, faltan en el manuscrito Chacón, y corrige en no pocas poesías la fecha que Chacón les diera.»

as his in this study, and to venture a hypothesis about why certain texts were selected and others passed over or not considered for inclusion in the Chacón manuscript.[10] Góngora's popularity and his striving for perfection help to explain his variants and to characterize his art as one of maturation.

Distinguishing the genuine from the apocryphal variants is a step towards determining the significance of Góngora's poems, because variants often change the meaning of texts. Extensive variants may even produce an entirely new or decidedly different version. Imitations are similar in style, theme, or both, and variants or versions that are not apocryphal may represent different stages of a poem's composition. Thus, a study of the variants, versions, and imitations of Góngora's poetry reveals the problems associated with his verse, explains the effects of these problems on his work, and offers insights into Góngora's creative process —three important goals applicable to much of the textual tradition of Spain's Golden Age poets.

---

[10] The present study deals only with Góngora's shorter poems; it does not treat the variants of El Polifemo and Las soledades because Dámaso Alonso and other scholars have already undertaken this task. See DÁMASO ALONSO, Góngora y el «Polifemo», 5th ed. (Madrid: Gredos, 1967), III, who analyzes —in detail— the variants of GÓNGORA's El Polifemo. PETER M. KOMANECKY, «The 'Primera soledad' of Don Luis de Góngora y Argote: An Edition with Commentary», unpubl. Ph. D. diss., The Johns Hopkins University, 1972, discusses the Chacón text of Góngora's «Primera soledad» (DAI, 33, n. 73 [May, 1973], 6360-A), comments on earlier versions of the poem, examines D. Alonso's modern prosification of it, and provides information on the interpretation and sources of Góngora's poetry. Some seventeenth-century critics who have commented on Góngora's Las soledades are Diego García de Salcedo Coronel, Pedro Díaz de Rivas, José Pellicer de Salas y Tovar, Andrés de Almansa y Mendoza, Juan de Jáuregui, Francisco Fernández de Córdoba, and Martín Vázquez Siruela.

II

MAJOR VARIANTS

A) The Five Endings of Góngora's «Servia en Oran al Rei»

The Chacón manuscript of Góngora's poetry includes a lengthy section of *romances*. Góngora's *romances nuevos,* like those of most Golden Age writers, were not often printed under the poet's name until after his death.[1] They were, instead, collected in general anthologies such as the *Romancero general* of 1600.[2] Because epico-lyric poetry was very much in vogue in the sixteenth and seventeenth centuries, it was much more accessible in print than other kinds of verse. Its broad circulation reflected the taste of the public and the prestige attributed to the genre by the erudite poets who imitated the *romances viejos.*[3]

One of Góngora's *romances* —the Moorish artistic ballad entitled 'Servia en Oran al Rei'— is known to exist in five versions. One of these was the Chacón text that received the poet's seal of approval:

> Servia en Oran al Rei
> Vn Hespañol con dos lanças,
> I con el alma i la vida
> A vna gallarda Africana,
> 5 Tan noble como hermosa,
> Tan amante como amada,
> Con quien estaba vna noche,
> Quando tocaron al arma.
> Trecientos Cenetes eran
> 10 De este rebato la causa,

¹ Rodríguez-Moñino, *Poesía y cancioneros (siglo XVI)* (Madrid: n.p., 1968), p. 19, comments on editions of poets' works: «Por lo que respecta a los volúmenes impresos con obra individual, hemos de decir ante todo que son escasísimos los poetas de la época que vieron estampadas sus tareas literarias.»

² Comp. Luis Sánchez (Madrid, 1600; facs. rpt. New York: De Vinne Press, 1904).

³ *Spanish Ballads,* ed. C. Colin Smith (Oxford: Pergamon, 1964), p. 18: «In the 16th and early 17th centuries the ballad prospered as did so much else in life and in art, in the great release of creative energies which we call the Renaissance and the Golden Age. Ballads of every type achieved enormous popularity among all classes; beloved of musicians, profitable to printers, esteemed by scholars, imitated eventually by the greatest poets of the age, known to all, they formed a unique national heritage.»

Que los raios de la Luna
Descubrieron sus adargas;
Las adargas auisaron
A las mudas atalaias,
15   Las atalaias los fuegos,
Los fuegos a las campanas;
I ellas al enamorado,
Que en los brazos de su Dama
Oyò el militar estruendo
20   De las trompas i las caxas.
Espuelas de honor le pican,
I freno de Amor le para:
No salir es couardia,
Ingratitud es dexalla.
25   Del cuello pendiente ella,
Viendole tomar la espada,
Con lagrimas i suspiros
Le dice aquestas palabras:
'Salid al campo, señor,
30   Bañen mis ojos la cama;
Que ella me serà tambien,
Sin vos, campo de batalla.
Vestìos i salid apriesa,
Que el General os aguarda,
35   Io os hago a vos mucha sobra
I vos a el mucha falta.
Bien podeis salir desnudo,
Pues mi llanto no os ablanda;
Que teneis de acero el pecho,
40   I no aueis menester armas.'
Viendo el Hespañol brioso
Quanto le detiene i habla,
Le dice assi: 'Mi señora,
Tan dulce como enojada,
45   Porque con honra i Amor
Io me quede, cumpla i vaia,
Vaia a los Moros el cuerpo,
I quede con vos el alma.
Concededme, dueño mio,
50   Licencia para que salga
Al rebato en vuestro nombre,
I en vuestro nombre combata.'

(CHACÓN: FOULCHÉ-DELBOSC, I, 95-96)[4]

---

[4] Throughout my study, I have translated the Chacón texts of Góngora's poems. My translation of «Servia en Oran al Rei» follows: In Oran a Spaniard was serving the king with two lances and, with his soul and his life, an elegant African girl, as noble as she was beautiful, as loving as she was loved, with whom he was spending one night when they sounded the call to battle. Three hundred Zenecha tribesmen were the cause of this summons, for the rays of the moon had discovered their shields; the shields warned the quiet watchtowers, the watchtowers the fires, the fires the bells, and the bells the lover, who, in his lady's arms, heard the military clamor of the

Like the other versions, this text tells the story of a Spaniard on military service in Oran sometime after its capture by Spain in 1509. In circumstances reminiscent of the courtly love tradition, the ballad's noble Christian is literally and metaphorically aroused from his lovemaking and summoned away from his beloved by the call to battle. While the Moorish girl mourns her sad fate, the narrator intervenes (41-44)[5] to prepare the reader for the soldier's response to his beloved:

> Viendo el Hespañol brioso
> Quanto le detiene i habla,
> Le dice assi: 'Mi señora,
> Tan dulce como enojada...
>
> (CHACÓN: FOULCHÉ-DELBOSC, I, 96)

This incomplete sentence constitutes the last quatrain assuredly written by Góngora, for Chacón notes that the poem's final two strophes are substitutions for the original six or seven that have been lost: «Estos dos vltimos quartetes [sic] son agenos, en lugar de otros seis o siete suios, que no se han podido hallar» (Foulché-Delbosc, I, 96).

A second version of the ballad, discovered by E. Herman Hespelt in 1930, is located in manuscript 10313 of the Nationalbibliothek in Vienna. In an article written in the same year, Hespelt described his find:

> The library catalogue, in its description of the manuscript, places it in the 17th century. As the manuscript is anonymous and its origin and sources unknown, it is difficult to vouch for the authenticity of its contents. The ballad must speak for itself. The scribe does not mention Góngora's name, nor does he indicate whether he copied the poem from a written or printed source or whether —as some of the variant passages seem to indicate— he wrote from memory.[6]

Juan and Isabel Millé point out a third version, which is incorporated in manuscript 4127 of the Biblioteca Nacional, and Foulché-Delbosc reproduced a fourth from a manuscript volume in the Biblioteca Brancacciana

---

trumpets and drums. The spurs of honor prick him, and the bridle of love restrains him; not to leave is cowardice, to abandon her is ingratitude. Hanging about his neck, seeing him take his sword, she speaks to him these words with tears and sighs: «Go out to the battlefield, sir; let my eyes bathe the bed, for, without you, it too will be a battlefield for me. Get dressed and leave quickly, because the general is expecting you; I am very unnecessary to you, and you are greatly needed by him. You can easily leave naked, for my weeping does not soften you, because you have a heart of steel, and you have no need for arms.» The courageous Spaniard, seeing how long she talks and detains him, speaks to her in this way: «My lady, as sweet as you are angry, in order that with honor and love I may stay, perform my duty, and depart, let my body go to the Moors, and let my soul stay with you. Grant me, my beloved, permission to go to the attack in your name and in your name to fight.»

[5] In my text, all numbers appearing alone between parentheses refer to lines.
[6] «A Variant of One of Góngora's Ballads», MLN, 45 (1930), 160.

(Naples).[7] A fifth version —found in the binding of a sixteenth-century book in the Biblioteca Provincial de Badajoz— has been published by Rodríguez-Moñino. The text of the poem was handwritten by don Gerónimo Flores de la Torre, possibly in the year 1587, the date assigned to this *romance* in the Chacón manuscript.[8]

Accepting Chacón's word that the conclusion he provides for the ballad is not authentic, one may speculate that, at the time of his collaboration with Chacón, Góngora did not have in his possession any of the endings of the versions found today in the libraries in Vienna, Madrid, Naples, and Badajoz, but that one of them may be his work. The ending as given in the five manuscript versions follows:

CHACÓN

Viendo el Hespañol brioso
Quanto le detiene i habla,
Le dice assi: 'Mi señora,
Tan dulce como enojada,
45 Porque con honra i Amor
Io me quede, cumpla i vaia,
Vaia a los Moros el cuerpo,
I quede con vos el alma.
Concededme, dueño mio,
50 Licencia para que salga
Al rebato en vuestro nombre,
I en vuestro nombre combata.'

(FOULCHÉ-DELBOSC, I, 96)

VIENNA

El galan que tiernamente
la escucha la mira y habla
le dize señora mia
tan dolçe como enojada
45 non illorejs [sic] ojos hermosos
que uestras lagrimas manchan
mis honrados piensamientos
y augueran mis esperanzas
por que con honra y amor
50 yo cumpla que me quede y vaya
uaya a los moros el cuerpo
y quede con uos el alma
que no uolueran a Oran

---

[7] LUIS DE GÓNGORA, *Obras completas,* ed. Juan Millé y Giménez and Isabel Millé y Giménez (Madrid: Aguilar, 1943), p. 1006; R. FOULCHÉ-DELBOSC, «Romancero de la Biblioteca Brancacciana», *RHi,* 65 (1925), 353.

[8] ANTONIO RODRÍGUEZ-MOÑINO, «El romance de Góngora 'Servía en Orán al Rey' (Textos y notas para su estudio)», in his *La transmisión de la poesía española en los siglos de oro,* ed. Edward M. Wilson (Barcelona: Ariel, 1976), pp. 20-21.

```
          sin catiuos y sin fama
     55   esta espada en uestro nombre
          a dios [sic] que tocan al arma.
```
(HESPELT, pp. 160-61)

MADRID

```
          El galán, que tiernamente,
          la escucha, la mira y ama,
          le responde: ¡Ay mi señora,
          tan dulce como enojada,
     45   porque con honra y honor [sic]
          yo cumpla, me quede y vaya,
          vaya a los moros el cuerpo
          y quede con vos el alma.
          No lloréis, ojos hermosos,
     50   que aquesas lágrimas manchan
          mis honrados pensamientos
          y quitan mis esperanzas.
          Vuestra gracia sola pida,
          que me será sola gracia,
     55   en las batallas escudo
          y en las vitorias guirnalda.
          Quedaos a Dios, mi señora
          y concededme que vaya,
          y el rebate [sic] en vuestro nombre,
     60   y en vuestro nombre combata,
          que no volveré de Orán
          sin cautivos ni sin fama,
          y esta espada en vuestro nombre,
          y adiós, que tocan al arma.
```
(MILLÉS, p. 1006)

NAPLES

```
          El galan que tiernamente
          la mira y escucha y habla,
          le rresponde: Mi señora,
     40   tan dulce como enoxada,
          para que con mas onor
          yo me quede, parta y uaya,
          uaya a los moros el cuerpo,
          y quede con vos el alma.
     45   Conçededme, mi señora,
          liçençia para que parta
          a combatir con los moros,
          y en vuestro nombre combata.
          Que no volveré a Oran
     50   sin cautiuos o sim [sic] palma
          esta espada en vuestro nombre,
          y adios, que tocan al arma.
```
(FOULCHÉ-DELBOSC, «Romancero», p. 353)

10

BADAJOZ

el galan que atentamente
se la mira escucha y ama
le responde mi señora
40   tan dulce quanto enojada
no lloren ojos ermosos
que aquesas lagrimas bastan
a borrar mis pensamientos
y a borrar mis esperanças
45   y pues con onrra y amor
conbiene que quede y baya
baya a los moros el cuerpo
y quede con bos el alma
solo una gracia os pido
50   que me sea uestra gracia
en las batallas escudo
y en las uictorias guirnalda
dadme uestra bendición
y permitidme que salga
55   al rrebato en uestro nonbre
y en uestro nonbre conbata.
que de no boluer a oran
sin victoria o sin el alma
este braço os lo promete
60   y adios mi bien que me llaman.

(RODRÍGUEZ-MOÑINO, «El romance», pp. 26-27)

The first noticeable difference between the conclusions lies in their initial lines. After pointing out the contention between the powerful demands of love and of military duty that have overcome the Spaniard, the Chacón text stresses the knight's valor and the priority, for him, of fighting for his country: «Viendo el Hespañol brioso/Quanto le detiene i habla...» (41-42). In the interpolated lines of «Vienna», «Madrid», «Naples», and «Badajoz» it is rather his compassion and courtliness toward the beloved that are accentuated: «El galan que tiernamente/la escucha la mira y habla» (41-42) («Vienna»), «El galán, que tiernamente,/la escucha, la mira y ama» (41-42) («Madrid»), «El galan que tiernamente/la mira y escucha y habla» (37-38) («Naples»), and «el galan que atentamente/se la mira escucha y ama» (37-38) («Badajoz»). Heroism has yielded to a lover's tenderness, and honor to sentimentality.

The final verses of «Vienna», «Madrid», and «Naples» are examples of Góngora's technique of merely alluding to events and hinting at results. In the last lines of the apocryphal Chacón text, the text leads the reader to surmise that the soldier is leaving his beloved to carry out his military obligation. The poet, however, never confirms the reader's hypothesis:

11

Concededme, dueño mio,
50   Licencia para que salga
Al rebato en vuestro nombre,
I en vuestro nombre combata.

This quatrain —slightly modified— is the penultimate one in «Madrid», but it is grammatically defective and does not make sense:

Quedaos a Dios, mi señora
y concededme que vaya,
y el rebate [sic] en vuestro nombre,
60   y en vuestro nombre combata.

«Naples» is most clearly related to «Chacón» in this strophe:

45   Conçededme, mi señora,
liçençia para que parta
a combatir con los moros,
y en vuestro nombre combata.

Its final quatrain, however, is similar to those of «Madrid» and «Vienna» because it informs the reader that the soldier abandons his beloved for honor's sake:

Que no volverè a Oran
50   sin cautiuos o sim [sic] palma
esta espada en vuestro nombre,
y adios, que tocan al arma.

The last lines of «Madrid» and «Vienna» read:

que no volveré de Orán
sin cautivos ni sin fama,
y esta espada en vuestro nombre,
y adios, que tocan al arma.[9]
(61-64)

que no uolueran a Oran[10]
sin catiuos y sin fama
55   esta espada en uestro nombre
a dios [sic] que tocan al arma.

[9] This quatrain, although grammatically sound, is logically defective. It can be read as follows: «que no volveré de Orán sin cautivos y fama, ni sin esta espada en vuestro nombre. Adiós, que tocan al arma.» Clearly, the copyist forgot that the Spaniard was already in Oran. Because the general theme of the poem is that the Spaniard leaves his beloved to fight the Moors, it was easy to assume (forgetting the beginning of the poem) that the knight was leaving Spain and going to fight in Africa.

[10] «Uolueran» must be either a scribal error for «volverá» or the author's mistake resulting from a lapse of attention because the subject of the verb can only be «esta espada».

The knight in the three versions proclaims he will fight with his sword in the name of his lady and not return to Oran without prisoners and either fame or victory. Anticipating the honor of his homecoming, he obviously hopes to be triumphant.

«Vienna» and «Madrid» may have replicated Góngora's missing lines, but their poor grammar and logic suggest that, at best, they are defective copies of the lost verses. If the minor variants contained in the body of the texts of «Madrid», «Naples», and «Vienna», however, were regarded by Góngora as inferior to those included in the Chacón manuscript, then perhaps the conclusions of these versions would also have been repudiated by the poet. Although corrupt endings may reflect authentic traditions, the last two quatrains of Chacón's version that are «agenos» are somewhat more acceptable than those of «Naples» and distinctly superior to the concluding strophes of «Vienna» and «Madrid».

Turning to «Badajoz», the reader finds that this text and that of «Madrid» fulfill Chacón's description of the *romance*'s missing strophes. Six or seven quatrains —according to Chacón— constitute the conclusion of the ballad; «Badajoz's» and «Madrid's» endings comprise exactly six. The «Badajoz» text is most like «Chacón» in that it has fewer minor variants than those included in «Naples», «Vienna», or «Madrid». «Badajoz's» final verses, however, are very closely related to those in the last strophes of «Madrid», except that they are grammatically sound. «Sea» in line 50 makes sense of the whole ending. Because the subjunctive is used throughout the conclusions of «Madrid» and «Badajoz», «sea» is the only conjugated form of the verb «to be» that completes the poem logically. The use of the future tense in the *romance*'s conclusion is not consistent with that of the verbs in the poem's preceding lines. The outcome of the soldier's military adventure as expressed by «sea» is unclear. «Será», on the other hand, suggests either future triumph or a very remote possibility of failure. The «Badajoz» ending is thus more indefinite than that of «Madrid». Its contrived ambiguity and correct grammar may well mean that it is Góngora's missing conclusion.

The discovery of the strophes that may comprise the authentic ending to «Servia en Oran al Rei» not only offers the reader a better understanding of the body of this *romance*, but also demonstrates how a conclusion finishes a poem in accordance with that work's grammar and theme. Moreover, the identification of the «Badajoz» verses of Góngora's poem as the *romance*'s possible missing lines contributes to the perfection and completion of the Chacón manuscript, the only official anthology of Góngora's poetry. Like «Servia en Oran al Rei», other poems lacking authentic conclusions are reproduced in the Chacón collection. My analysis of «Servia en Oran al Rei» suggests the possibility of finding the lost endings to these Góngora poems, as in the case of the lyrical *letrilla* discussed in the follow-

13

ing section of this chapter, and to texts by other Spanish Golden Age poets.

B) The Effect of Truncation on the «Letrilla» «No son todos ruiseñores»

Another poem, Góngora's lyrical *letrilla*, «No son todos ruiseñores», is known to exist in two versions that are the same except for their endings. One version, the Chacón text as approved by Góngora, is an apocopated form of the other as reproduced by Robert Jammes.[11] The Chacón text is as follows:

No son todos ruiseñores
Los que cantan entre las flores,
Sino campanitas de plata,
    Que tocan a la Alua;
5 Sino trompeticas de oro,
    Que hacen la salua
A los Soles que adoro.[12]

No todas las voces ledas
Son de Syrenas con plumas,
10 Cuias humidas espumas
Son las verdes alamedas.
Si suspendido te quedas
A los súaues clamores,
No son todos ruiseñores
15 Los que cantan entre las flores,
Sino campanitas de plata
    Que tocan a la Alua,
Sino trompeticas de oro
    Que hacen la salua
20 A los Soles que adoro.

Lo artificioso que admira,
I lo dulce que consuela,
No es de aquel violin que vuela
Ni de esotra inquieta lyra;
25 Otro instrumento es quien tira
De los sentidos mejores:

---

[11] In *Letrillas* (Paris: Ediciones Hispano-Americanas, 1963), p. 9, Jammes says that the poem has a third strophe that appears in six manuscripts. Jammes rescued this strophe from oblivion and used it to interpret the rest of the difficult and elusive text.

[12] Góngora's refrain, reminiscent of the *poesía de tipo tradicional*, is sung in the «danza de los palos»: «No son todas palomitas / las que pican en el montón; / no son todas palomitas, / que algunos palomitos son.» In the twentieth century, this song has been collected by Eduardo M. Torner. See his *Lírica hispánica* (Madrid: Castalia, 1966), p. 293.

No son todos ruiseñores
Los que cantan entre las flores,
Sino campanitas de plata,
30   Que tocan a la Alua,
Sino trompeticas de oro
Que hacen la salua
A los Soles que adoro.

(CHACÓN: FOULCHÉ-DELBOSC, I, 321-22)[13]

In its shortened version, the *letrilla* appears to deal with a major aesthetic issue of Góngora's lifetime by suggesting that artistic beauty is at least as important as natural beauty. The recently exhumed third strophe, however, considered by scholars to be Góngora's work, sheds new light on the interpretation of the universal problem of the art-nature conflict:

Las campanitas luzientes,
35   y los dorados clarines
en coronados jazmines,
los dos hermosos corrientes
no sólo recuerdan gentes
sino convocan amores.
40   No son todos ruiseñores
los que cantan entre las flores,
sino campanitas de plata,
que tocan a la Alva;
sino trompeticas de oro,
45   que hacen la salva
a los Soles que adoro.

(JAMMES, p. 8)[14]

With the recovery of the poem's conclusion and the consequent increased understanding of the *letrilla,* a question arises: Why did Góngora omit the

---

[13] I have translated this *letrilla* here: Not all are nightingales that sing among the flowers, but little silver bells which serenade the dawn, but tiny golden trumpets which play a fanfare to the suns (eyes) that I adore. Not all the joyful voices come from feathered syrens whose damp sea foams are the green poplar groves. If you remain entranced by the delicate cries, not all are nightingales that sing among the flowers, but little silver bells which serenade the dawn, but tiny golden trumpets which play a fanfare to the suns (eyes) that I adore. The artistry that you admire and the sweetness that soothes you come not from that flying violin, nor from this other restless lyre; it is another instrument that plays on your better senses: not all are nightingales that sing among the flowers, but little silver bells which serenade the dawn, but tiny golden trumpets which play a fanfare to the suns (eyes) that I adore. The little shining bells, and the golden trumpets on crowned jasmines, the two beautiful streams, not only awaken people, but summon lovers. Not all are nightingales that sing among the flowers, but little silver bells which serenade the dawn, but tiny golden trumpets which play a fanfare to the suns (eyes) that I adore.

[14] JAMMES, p. 9, makes the following statements about his sources: «Les éditions et la plupart des manuscrits ne donnent que les deux premières strophes. La troisième se trouve dans BL, E, I, K, NB, RM.» His abbreviations stand for six manuscripts that he describes on pp. 487-88, 489, 490, 491, 492, and 495, respectively. JAMMES, p. 9, notes the poem's variants.

third strophe from the Chacón collection of his poetry?[15] An analysis of the *letrilla* and of the effects the addition or omission of the final strophe have on it suggest a probable answer to this question.

In the first two strophes of each version, the songs of nightingales and other birds are accompanied by the sounds of trumpets and bells that enhance natural beauty with their artistic tones. Nature assumes the form of art (musical instruments), however, as the poet metamorphosizes the birds in the *letrilla:* «aquel violin que vuela» and «esotra inquieta lyra».[16] It is axiomatic that nature's harmony is soft and melodious, but «Otro instrumento es quien tira/De los sentidos mejores». Because the poet fails to identify the unknown instrument whose song is so sweet that it exceeds even that of nature, scholars have only been able to guess at its identity. Some may surmise that the instrument is love or beauty, and some have specifically held that Góngora's love for Cloris (doña Brianda de la Cerda) may have been the inspiration for this poem as it was for several written from 1606-08.[17]

The reader's problematic understanding of the *letrilla*'s two strophes is elucidated by the addition of the third. He learns from the final verses that nature's symphony has been expanded and the force of the antithesis has been mitigated. The two artistic instruments, «trompeticas» and «campanitas», are now understood to be symbols of natural beauty —buzzing bees and running water:

> ... parmi les rumeurs de l'aube, le poète nous invite à écouter, non le chant des oiseaux, devenu banal, mais des bruits plus humbles et plus riches à la fois: le bourdonnement des abeilles («trompeticas de oro») qui butinent le jasmin, le bruit cristallin du ruisseau («campanitas de plata») qui coule parmi les fleurs. (JAMMES, p. 10)

Each version of the *letrilla* thus exerts its metaphoric powers over the reader. The last verse of the poem's refrain, for example, includes the metaphor, «Soles», a reference to the eyes of the poet's beloved. The word «adoro» suggests that the lady, symbolized by the «Soles», represents divine, in addition to earthly, beauty that radiates amidst nature as the musical instruments (bees and water) play a fanfare for her.

The *letrilla* is a type of *alba* poem summoning lovers from their sleep so they may have the opportunity for lovemaking surrounded by all the natural elegance of a rural morning. The metaphors involving the sun and birds, suggestive of poetry in the Petrarchan tradition, are part of Gón-

---

[15] It is possible that, at the time of the manuscript's compilation, Góngora had misplaced the third strophe. I believe, however, that, in this case, he may have deliberately suppressed the verses for artistic purposes as discussed in the remainder of this chapter's section B.

[16] Cf. ALONSO, *Góngora y El «Polifemo»*, II, 113.

[17] JAMMES, p. 11.

gora's artistic technique employed to enhance the beauty of nature. The poet describes a scene in which the reader's senses extend beyond the realm of reality to a world of illusion. There the reader becomes intoxicated by the natural setting conjured up by Góngora's verses, and art (the musical symphony) is transformed into nature (the birds, bees, and stream) and nature (the woodland setting) into art (the poem).

The power of metaphor, however, is only part of this *letrilla*'s true poetic artistry, which lies chiefly in the mystique created by its truncation. Like the short version of the «Romance del Conde Arnaldos», which Menéndez Pidal argued to be aesthetically superior to the fifteenth-century long version (which he discovered among the Sephardim of Morocco[18]), the abbreviated version of Góngora's *letrilla* loses its charm with the addition of the poem's final verses. The identification of the «campanitas» and «trompeticas» as part of nature's symphony has effectively resolved the reader's dilemma concerning the art-nature conflict; there are no longer two forces —artistic and natural beauty— vying against each other.

The unidentified instruments of Góngora's short version possess the same power of attraction as does the mariner's song in the truncated *romance*. The sailor's mysterious song entices Arnaldos to board the galley, just as the instruments in Góngora's poem lure the reader into the *letrilla*'s poplar groves. There, the music of nature —of the «campanitas» and «trompeticas» and of the other, yet unidentified, instrument— fills the air. The wondrous concert in the woods is suggestive of the poetry of Fray Luis de León, of the harmony of the spheres, as well as of the many supernatural poems from international folklore[19] that —like the mariner's song— evoke the age-old mysteries of the universe.

As the reader of the abbreviated *romance* is engulfed by the melody of an unfathomable sea tune, so the reader of the short *letrilla* is surrounded by the enchantment of a forest awakening to the sounds of spring. The allure of these truncated versions, however, is destroyed by the addition of more lines. The final verses of the long *romance* —in which the count reveals his true identity and learns that of the ship's sailors who have been searching for him[20] —cause the Moroccan version to sink into the depths

---

[18] RAMÓN MENÉNDEZ PIDAL, «Poesía popular y poesía tradicional en la literatura española», in *Los romances de América y otros estudios,* 6th ed. (Buenos Aires: Austral, 1958), pp. 64-65: «Se notará ahora que esta forma en que el poeta primitivo concibió el romance de 'Arnaldos', con ser estimable, vale mucho menos que aquella en que el romance fue truncado, tal como se imprimió en el Cancionero de Amberes hacia 1545.» Whereas the truncated version of this traditional ballad ends with a thought-provoking line sung to the Count Arnaldos by the mariner of an approaching galley: «'Yo no digo esta canción / sino a quien conmigo va'» (p. 59), Menéndez Pidal's twentieth-century Moroccan find goes on to answer the question.

[19] LEO SPITZER, «The Folkloristic Pre-stage of the Spanish *Romance* 'Count Arnaldos'», *HR,* 23 (1955), 185.

[20] In the Moroccan version, the reader discovers that the count is really a French

17

of banality, where it becomes merely one more *romance novelesco*.[21] The same effect holds true for Góngora's *letrilla*. Because its last strophe discloses the metaphorical meaning of the «campanitas» and «trompeticas», the reader no longer needs to ask: 1) what do these instruments symbolize?, 2) what is their relationship to nature or art?, or 3) how do they affect the meaning of the *letrilla*?

Some of the appeal of Góngora's poem, however, depends on the unidentified «otro instrumento» «quien tira/De los sentidos mejores» that, as previously stated, alludes to more than the natural beauty encountered in the poplar groves. Whether «quien» refers to God, woman, love, beauty, or art, or whether it refers to someone or something else, that it is «otro instrumento» that plays on the «sentidos mejores» keeps the reader wondering: 1) what are the «better senses»?, 2) how does the instrument play on them?, and, of course, 3) what is the instrument? The real artistic beauty of «No son todos ruiseñores» thus lies mostly in its truncated form and partly in the unsolved puzzle of the «otro instrumento».

The issue of truncation, illustrated by this *letrilla*, arises in discussions of much Golden Age poetry. In particular, another Góngora poem, «Entre los sueltos cauallos», comes to mind. This *romance*, which exists in both a short and a long version, was published in its short form in the Chacón manuscript.[22] The long text appears in the Vicuña edition of Góngora's works (p. 78). The principal difference between the Vicuña and Chacón texts, as pointed out by Albert E. Sloman in his article, «The Two Versions of Góngora's 'Entre los sueltos caballos'», is the addition of forty anticlimactic lines in the Vicuña version.[23] It is possible that these forty lines, although reproduced as Góngora's by Vicuña, are not by the poet. However, in other cases involving the doubtful authenticity of verses, the Chacón manuscript includes the questionable lines with a note that either they are probably not by Góngora or that they are apocryphal verses replacing lost lines. The Chacón manuscript, however, does not mention the forty verses. Furthermore, most modern editors reproduce the long text.[24]

prince and the galley a French vessel that has been looking for him. See MENÉNDEZ PIDAL, p. 64.

[21] MENÉNDEZ PIDAL, p. 69: «Bien acabamos de ver cómo las más antiguas y autorizadas versiones del 'Arnaldos', que nos cuentan lógica y redondeadamente los peligros del mar y sus venturas son evidentemente muy inferiores a la versión trunca y contaminada recogida en el Cancionero de Amberes.»

[22] See FOULCHÉ-DELBOSC, I, 75-77.

[23] See SLOMAN, *RFE*, 44 (1961), 436-37. SLOMAN, pp. 438-39, notes that the long text also appears in the Hoces edition of Góngora's poetry (fols. 81v-82v). The Hoces version is essentially the same as that of Vicuña except for minor variants, a few new readings, and two new quatrains. Where the Vicuña and Chacón versions diverge, the Hoces text sometimes follows that of Chacón, but the biggest difference between the Hoces and Vicuña versions is that the quatrain with which the Chacón text ends is transferred to the end of the Hoces version where it does not make sense.

[24] See SLOMAN, p. 438, and José M. Cossío, *Romances de Góngora* (Madrid: RO,

Although Sloman (p. 441) believes the verses are of doubtful origin, Góngora may have written these lines, which were later corrupted by copyists before their inclusion in Vicuña. Góngora may have omitted the original verses from the Chacón anthology because he could not find a copy of them at the time of the manuscript's compilation, or he may have suppressed them for artistic purposes, as was probably the case with the third strophe of «No son todos ruiseñores».

Similarly, Góngora altered or deleted strophes or endings of his satirical *letrillas*, poems that often took the form of catalogues of vices and follies, to avoid censure or censorship or to expand his criticism of society. Many of these *letrillas*, such as «Vn buhonero ha empleado» discussed in the next part of this chapter, have truncation or omitted strophes.

C) VARIANT STROPHES AND STROPHIC ORDER IN «VN BUHONERO HA EMPLEADO»

Each strophe of the *letrilla* «Vn buhonero ha empleado» is a separate satire of a stereotyped member of Spanish Golden Age society, and each may be omitted or retained, altering the ending or other part of the poem without changing the work's overall meaning. All of the strophes conclude with a cardinal number followed by the word «higa(s)» that together form a refrain. A «higa» is both a gesture of scorn, represented by a fist with the thumb sticking out between the middle and index fingers, and an amulet, in the form of this gesture, worn to protect oneself from evil.[25] Underlining the faults of various members of society as portrayed in the *letrilla*, the refrain suggests that these individuals should be jeered at for their behavior and that they need a peddler's amulets to protect them from vice. The order of the poem's strophes is relatively unimportant except that the number of «higas» increases with every succeeding strophe, perhaps with what the poet may have considered to be the more serious offenses.

«Vn buhonero ha empleado» exists in widely different versions. The four most accepted and significant of these are discussed here.[26] In the

---

1927), pp. 41-44. Cossío, p. 44, comments that the additional verses are of debatable authenticity, but he reproduces them «porque en todas las ediciones figuran».

[25] See the *Diccionario de la lengua castellana* (Madrid: RAE, 1726-39), facs. *Diccionario de Autoridades* (Madrid: Gredos, 1963), II, pt. 4, p. 154, s.v. «higa». See also SEBASTIÁN DE COVARRUBIAS HOROZCO, *Tesoro de la lengua castellana o española* (Madrid: Luis Sánchez, 1611), facs. with the additions of Benito Remingo Noydens that were published in the 1674 edition, ed. Martín de Riquer (Barcelona: Horta, 1943), p. 689, s.v. «higa».

[26] Besides the four versions discussed here, Góngora's poem is included in twenty-six other sources in which the order, omission, or addition of strophes one to fourteen varies (see JAMMES, p. 79). JAMMES, pp. 81-83, lists several sources of Góngora's *letrilla* and the variants found in each of them.

3

Chacón manuscript, the *letrilla,* dated 1593, is composed of ten strophes that satirize only men:

Vn buhonero ha empleado
En higas oi su caudal,
I aunque no son de crystal,
Todas las ha despachado;
5   Para mi le he demandado,
Quando verdades no diga,
   Vna higa.

Al necio, que le dan pena
Todos los agenos daños,
10   I aunque sea de cien años,
Alcança vista tan buena,
Que vee la paja en la agena
I no en la suia dos vigas,
   Dos higas.

15   Al otro, que le dan jaque
Con vna Dama atreguada,
I mas bien pelotéàda
Que la Coruña del Draque,
I fiada del çumaque,
20   Le desmiente tres barrigas,
   Tres higas.

Al marido, que es ia llano
Sin dar vn marauedi,
Que le hinche el alholi
25   Su muger cada Verano,
Si piensa que grano a grano
Se lo llegan las hormigas,
   Quatro higas.

Al que pretende mas saluas
30   I ceremonias maiores
Que se deben por Señores
A los Infantados i Aluas,
Siendo nacido en las maluas
I criado en las hortigas,
35   Cinco higas.

Al pobre pelafustan
Que de arrogancia se paga,
I presenta la bisnaga
Por testigo del faisan,
40   Viendo que las barbas dan
Testimonio de las migas,
   Seis higas.

Al que de sedas armado,
Tal para Cadiz camina,
45   Que ninguno determina

20

Si es vandera o si es soldado,
De su voluntad forçado,
Llorado de sus amigas,
    Siete higas.

50 Al moçuelo, que en cambrai,
En purpura i en olores,
Quiere imitar sus maiores,
De quien oi memorias ai
Que los saios de contrai
55 Afforraban en lorigas,
    Ocho higas.

Al brabo que hecha de vicio,
I en los corrillos blasona
Que mil vidas amontona
60 A la muerte en sacrificio,
No tiniendo del officio
Mas que mostachos i ligas,
    Nuebe higas.

Al pretendiente engañado,
65 Que puesto que nada alcança,
Da pistos a la esperança
Quando mas desesperado,
Figurando ia granado
El fruto de sus espigas,
70   Diez higas.

(CHACÓN: FOULCHÉ-DELBOSC, I, 158-61)[27]

27 «Vn buhonero ha empleado» translates as follows: A peddler has invested his wealth in amulets today, and although they are not made of crystal, he has sold all of them. I demanded from him for myself, when I don't tell the truth, one amulet. For the fool, who feels sorry about other people's losses, and although he may be a hundred years old, he has such keen sight that he sees the straw in another's eye and not two beams in his own, two amulets. For the other, to whom they give a saddle-bag with a foolish lady better prostituted than Drake's Coruña, and she, trustful of the abortive drink, conceals three pregnancies, three amulets. To the married man, for whom it is already clear, without paying one gold coin, that his wife inflates the granary every summer, if he thinks that the ants are carrying it off grain by grain, four amulets. To the one who claims more salutes and major ceremonies than are owed to lords, princes, and the Dukes of Alba, having been born to humble lineage and raised in the lower class, five amulets. To the unfortunate vagabond, who takes a fancy to arrogance and who presents the toothpick as evidence of the pheasant, seeing that his whiskers give attestation to the crumbs, six amulets. To the man adorned with silks, who walks to Cadiz in such a way that no one can tell if he is a banner or a soldier, forced by his will, mourned by his lady friends, seven amulets. To the young fellow, who, in white linen, purple cloth, and perfumes, wants to imitate his elders from whom today there are memories that loose coats of fine cloth were lined with coats of mail, eight amulets. To the bully, who brags, and in coteries boasts, that he has given a thousand lives as a sacrifice to death, not possessing, for such a trade, more than moustaches and garters, nine amulets. To the deceived office-hunter, who, although he achieves nothing, nourishes hope when most desperate, pretending already choice the fruits of his thorns, ten amulets.

21

Whereas the Vicuña edition includes the poem as it appears in the Chacón manuscript,[28] the Hoces version (fol. 69r-v) replaces strophes nine and ten of the Chacón text with the following additional lines:

> A la viuda de Siqueo,
> sino es ya de regadio,
> pues calienta el lecho frio,
> 60 con suspiros del deseo,
> ya que son a lo que creo,
> por buenas sus fatigas
> nueue higas.
>
> (HOCES, fol. 69v)

«Vn buhonero ha empleado», also found in the *Romancero general* (1604), has eight strophes —seven from the Chacón version (numbers one, two, three, five, four, seven, and six, respectively) plus the extra verses beginning «A la viuda de Siqueo» that intervene between the fifth and fourth Chacón strophes.[29] This version, except for minor variants, is the one printed in the *Laberinto amoroso* (1618).[30] In both of these collections, the *letrilla* begins with the verse «*Ha* un buhonero empleado»,[31] and is composed of the same strophes in the same order.

Jammes, in his modern edition of Góngora's *letrillas,* prints a fourteen-strophe version of the poem (pp. 75-78).[32] He comments that ten of the poem's strophes, those constituting the Chacón version, must be by Góngora because the poet allowed them to be included in the Chacón manuscript; unlike apocryphal verses reproduced by Chacón, the ten strophes appear without any note that they are not by Góngora.[33] Jammes also mentions Dámaso Alonso's discussion of the *letrilla* as it figures in a manuscript of Góngora's poetry originally owned by José Pérez de Rivas, a poet from Córdoba who was a contemporary and admirer of Góngora.[34] In his

---

[28] See VICUÑA, p. 66.

[29] (Madrid: Juan de la Cuesta), in the *Romancero general 1600, 1604, 1605,* ed. Angel González Palencia, Clásicos Españoles, III-IV (Madrid: CSIC, 1947), II, 120-21.

[30] Ed. Juan de Chen (Barcelona: Sebastián de Cormellas, 1618), vignette ed. Karl Vollmöller in *RF,* 6 (1891), 128-29.

[31] The italics are mine.

[32] Jammes does not specifically mention the source of this version of Góngora's poem. Clearly, strophes one to ten are available in Foulché-Delbosc's edition of the Chacón manuscript, and strophe twelve is easily accessible in the *Romancero general* and the *Laberinto amoroso.* JAMMES, p. 79, lists strophes eleven, thirteen, and fourteen as included in Góngora's version of the *letrilla* in «BF» — Böhl de Faber's seventeenth-century manuscript, number 861 in the Biblioteca Nacional of Madrid (see JAMMES, p. 487).

[33] See JAMMES, p. 79, and FOULCHÉ-DELBOSC, I, 158-61.

[34] JAMMES, p. 80. See also DÁMASO ALONSO, «Puño y letra de don Luis en un manuscrito de sus poesías», in *Estudios y ensayos gongorinos* (Madrid: Gredos, 1955), who identifies Pérez de Rivas (pp. 252-53) and who notes that the poet is also known as Rivas Tafur and Pérez de Rivas Tafur (pp. 255-57). Although unlikely, it is not inconceivable that Pérez de Rivas might have been Pedro Díaz de Rivas, the scholar and priest who supported Góngora in the literary circles of Córdoba. However, it is

«Puño y letra de don Luis en un manuscrito de sus poesías», Alonso first notes that, in the Pérez de Rivas manuscript, Góngora not only corrected his own poems, but he rejected some in part and others completely (p. 251). Alonso later explains:

> Algunos (por lo menos) de los cuadernillos que formaron este manuscrito estuvieron en manos de Góngora, y el gran poeta puso en ellos correcciones y anotaciones de su puño y letra. (p. 254)

One of the poems that underwent Góngora's scrutiny was «Vn buhonero ha empleado». After consulting the same manuscript, Jammes notes that, following the strophe beginning «Al pretendiente engañado» (the tenth in the Chacón version and the eighth in the Jammes text), Góngora wrote:

> Faltan otras 4 o 5, y vnas q̃ comiençan *Al q̃ de vno al otro Polo, Al q̃ con ansia mortal, Al q̃ es de Toro maestro,* no son de el Sᵒʳ d. [L]uis de Góngora. (p. 79)

The three apocryphal strophes mentioned here are numbers eleven, thirteen, and fourteen, respectively, in the Jammes version of the *letrilla*:

11

Al que del uno al otro polo
es la hez de los poetas,
y quiere tener sujetas
las nueve hermanas de Apolo,
75   y que a no ser por él solo,
fueran las pobres mendigas,
onze higas.

13

85   Al que con ansia mortal
y encumbrados pensamientos,
anda beviendo los vientos
por dexar fama inmortal,
porque no le hagan mal
90   tantos vientos y fatigas,
treze higas.

14

Al que es Dotor o Maestro
de cualquiera Facultad,
y echa toldo y gravedad

more plausible that the two men were related. Both lived in Córdoba, composed verse, admired Góngora's poetry, and died in or around 1654. The Pérez de Rivas manuscript, which had a series of owners after Pérez de Rivas, was, according to Alonso, eventually acquired by the poet Joaquín Montaner, who first lent it to Alonso (p. 251). This critic again consulted it, when it was in the possession of Arturo Sedó, a collector of plays (the manuscript included a fragment of GÓNGORA's *Las firmezas de Isabela*) (p. 252).

95   teniéndose por más diestro,
       pudiéndole echar cabestro,
       y trabas en vez de ligas,
          treinta higas.

(JAMMES, pp. 77-78)

Strophe twelve is the one beginning «A la viuda de Siqueo».

There is some controversy concerning the authenticity of Góngora's strophes. Jammes (p. 80) explains that Alonso («Puño», pp. 260-61) believes that the third strophe, «Al otro, que le dan jaque», and the fourth, «Al marido, que es ia llano», as they appear in the Chacón manuscript, were late additions and that strophes nine and ten of the Chacón text —«Al brabo que hecha de vicio» and «Al pretendiente engañado»— are not by Góngora. Alonso notes that in the Pérez de Rivas manuscript the third and fourth strophes are missing and that Góngora had drawn two horizontal lines after the sixth strophe, «Al moçuelo que en Cambrai», and before the succeeding strophe, «Al brabo que echa de vicio» (strophes eight and nine, respectively, in the Chacón version). According to Alonso, Góngora wrote «no son mía[s] las que se sig[uen]» after these lines, when the *cuadernillo* was still unbound. Much later, the bookbinder, careless when sewing the pages together, covered the «s» of «mías» and the final letters of «siguen». Thus Alonso concludes that «no son mía[s] las que se sig[uen]», following strophe six and adjacent to strophe seven of the poem in Pérez de Rivas's manuscript (after strophe eight and next to strophe nine in the Chacón text), referred to strophes seven and eight in the Pérez de Rivas version (strophes nine and ten in the Chacón text) (Alonso, «Puño», pp. 260-61). Jammes (p. 80), however, understands that Góngora's words in the Pérez de Rivas manuscript were aimed at strophes on the opposite page, which was later torn out. Considering the previously mentioned note, «Faltan otras 4 o 5 ...», Jammes concludes that the first of the apocryphal strophes was «Al q̃ de vno al otro Polo», the eleventh of the version in his edition. He likewise deduces that «A la viuda de Siqueo», the twelfth strophe of the same text, was probably not written by Góngora, first because the poet disavowed it when compiling the Chacón manuscript, and second because it was readily accessible in the *Romancero general* (1604) and in the *Laberinto amoroso* (1618) (Jammes, p. 80).

It appears that Jammes is correct in determining that Góngora's words in the Pérez de Rivas manuscript were aimed at strophes on a page that had been torn out. Strophes one to ten in the Chacón manuscript, then, are surely Góngora's work. Whether the strophes noted as missing by Góngora are the same as the strophes numbered eleven to fourteen in Jammes's edition of Góngora's poetry is unclear.

Góngora's *letrilla* was widely circulated and scribes and poets added or deleted strophes as they saw fit, perhaps to censure people, perhaps

to censor verses, or perhaps to include strophes they believed authentic and to ignore others they considered spurious. Interestingly, the seventeenth-century compiler, Hoces, and some later editors such as Agustín Durán and Adolfo de Castro may have thought like Alonso. They reproduced strophes one to eight in the Chacón manuscript plus the strophe «A la viuda de Siqueo» found in Hoces's and Jammes's editions.[35] Some modern editors, such as the Millés (pp. 250-51), adhered loyally to the Chacón manuscript by reproducing strophes one to ten in Chacón's anthology and omitting the dubious strophe «A la viuda de Siqueo». In addition, critics and anthologists generally seemed to ignore or be unaware of the other three supposedly apocryphal strophes, numbered eleven, thirteen, and fourteen in the Jammes version of Góngora's letrilla, which may be Góngora's work. Thus the poem, a series of vignettes of society's members, has ten authentic and four questionable strophes. The text is open-ended, and the work's concluding verses are merely a function of the addition or omission of strophes.

Like «Vn buhonero ha empleado», many Golden Age poems are catalogues of vices and follies, and their strophic order can be changed without affecting the meaning of the text. Strophes can be added to the poems to increase criticism of social groups or of one's enemies, or strophes can be deleted to avoid censure or censorship. These reasons for omission and addition apply to some of Góngora's other poems such as «Dineros son calidad» and «Allà daràs, raio». Each strophe of both poems is a separate and complete representation of some regrettably fashionable aspect of everyday life. One strophe of «Dineros son calidad» is absent from the text of the poem published in Hoces's edition of Góngora's poetry. Like «Dineros son calidad», «Allà daràs, raio» appears without all of its verses in this edition. The omission may have been an oversight by either the editor or a copyist, but it was more likely a deliberate act of censorship, as proposed by Jammes.[36] Alfonso Reyes concurs with Jammes because he includes this poem, in addition to «Dineros son calidad», in his list of those tampered with by editors or censors.[37] The number of strophes in each version, however, is not important because it does not change the meaning of the poems. As illustrated in «Vn buhonero ha empleado», this technique of adding or deleting strophes was common in the Spanish Golden Age.

---

[35] See M. RIVADENEYRA, ed., Poetas líricos de los siglos XVI y XVII, Vol. XXXII of the BAE (Madrid: M. Rivadeneyra, 1854), p. 492, and AGUSTÍN DURÁN, Cancionero y romancero (Madrid: E. Aguado, 1829), p. 123.

[36] JAMMES, p. 110.

[37] REYES, pp. 84-85.

III

CLOSE VERSIONS AND IMITATIONS

A) «GRANDES MAS QUE ELEPHANTES I QUE HABADAS»:
A REFLECTION OF AN EARLIER VERSION OF THE
ELEPHANT/RHINOCEROS SONNET

In the Golden Age, versions of a known poem may have been imitations by one or more writers or earlier or later drafts by the same author. Whereas some such texts in existence today have many similar lines or strophes, others are almost completely different. Because the dates of variant texts are usually not accessible to the reader, it is often impossible to follow the stages of development of a poem or its versions. Gaining insight into a poet's creative process as reflected in the amending and improving of the original work is likewise difficult.

The versions of Góngora's sonnet «Grandes mas que elephantes i que habadas», however, offer the reader such unusual opportunities. A careful analysis of available data establishes the dates of the sonnet's texts within very narrow margins, and a study of their differences shows the remarkable improvement the poem experienced through witty and sardonic revisions.

The two versions of the sonnet are as follows:

I

Descrip[ç]am de Madrid.

Grandes mas q̃ elefantes y Abbadas
titulos liberales como rochas
gentiles hombres solo de las bocas
Discrete [sic] caualier llaues doradas
5 Habitos pleitos cambios embaixadas
confussa multitud de damas locas
carro[ç]as de ocho bestias y son pocas
con las q̃ las tiran y que son tiradas
Cata riberas animas en pena
10 con Bartolos m'es dada la milicia
y los derechos con espada y capa
Casas y pechos todo a la malicia

26

todos con pereel [sic] y hierua buena
dichoso el hombre q̃ de si se escapa.

II

Grandes mas que elephantes i que habadas,
Titulos liberales como rocas,
Gentiles hombres, solo de sus vocas,
Illustri Cauaglier, llaues doradas;
5   Habitos, capas digo remendadas,
Damas de haz i enues, viudas sin tocas,
Carroças de ocho bestias, i aun son pocas
Con las que tiran i que son tiradas;
Catarriberas, animas en pena,
10   Con Bartulos i Abbades la milicia,
I los derechos con espada i daga;
Casas i pechos todo a la malicia,
Lodos con peregil i ierbabuena:
Esto es la Corte. Buena prò les haga.[1]

The first, infiltrated by Portuguese orthographic and phonological variants, is included in Arthur Lee-Francis Askins's modern edition of the *Cancioneiro de corte e de magnates*; this Portuguese manuscript, originally published between 1608 and 1610, includes poems dating from the second half of the fifteenth to the first part of the seventeenth century.[2] Góngora's sonnet appears near the end of the *cancioneiro,* among various texts relating to poets and historical events that took place sometime around the early 1600s.[3]

The second version of «Grandes mas que elephantes i que habadas» is dated 1588 in the Chacón manuscript.[4] In spite of the general reliability of Góngora's official canon, it is not flawless, and the sonnet's assigned date is questionable; Joaquín de Entrambasaguas and Alonso have each

---

[1] «Grandes mas que elephantes i que habadas» translates as follows: Greater than elephants and rhinoceroses, titled men generous as rocks, the king's servants providing for only their own mouths, illustrious knights, golden keys, military robes, that is patched cloaks, two-faced ladies, widows without bonnets, carriages of eight beasts, and even they are few, including those that pull and those that are pulled, magistrates, souls in suffering, with jurisconsultants and the militia, and rights with a sword and dagger, houses and intentions all out of malice, mud with parsley and peppermint: this is the Court. May they (the nobles) profit from it.

[2] University of California Publications in Modern Philology, No. 84 (Berkeley: University of California Press, 1968). Askins discusses the date of the collection (p. 8) and reproduces the text of the sonnet (p. 10).

[3] ASKINS, p. 10: «Na última parte do MS, porém, há numerosas poesias que são da primeira parte do século XVII. Certas destas mostram claramente que os escribas estavam transcrevendo textos ainda nos anos 1607/1608. E vistas estas considerações em conjunto, ficamos com a convicção de que a época da terminação do códice foi pouco depois desta data, digamos 1608-1610.»

[4] See FOULCHÉ-DELBOSC, I, 106-07. In LUIS DE GÓNGORA, *Sonetos,* ed. Biruté Ciplijauskaité (Madison: HSMS, 1981), the poem appears on pp. 319-23, with mention of all manuscript and printed versions and an exhaustive apparatus of textual variants.

noted that the poet was not in Madrid until 1589-90.[5] Artigas, in his biography of Góngora, concurs, citing 1589 as the year in which the poet visited the capital city.[6] Jammes and Juan Millé, on the other hand, saw no problem with the date, 1588, based on a hypothetical journey to Madrid. Moreover, Góngora could have been writing from hearsay about the Court at Madrid or about any Court because this theme was quite trite by his day. Nevertheless, Jammes and Millé are most likely mistaken, and the conjecture that Góngora wrote from hearsay is not probable because the poet made several turn-of-the-century trips to Madrid, during or after any one of which he could have written the sonnet.[7]

Further pertinent information complicates the issue of chronology. First, Chacón confirms that when Góngora took part in compiling the Chacón manuscript, at the end of his lifetime, he dated his texts from memory, a difficult task for any prolific writer.[8]

Second, as mentioned before and as pointed out by Alfonso Reyes in his *Cuestiones gongorinas,* the Chacón manuscript, although authentic, is not without defects: «el propio manuscrito de Chacón, con ser la colección más autorizada, deja vivos todavía algunos problemas» (p. 41). Perhaps more confusing, however, is the historical notation that the sonnet was written to commemorate Philip II's receipt of the gift of one elephant and one rhinoceros from the governor of Java in 1581:

> En el reinado de Felipe II, año de 1581, se trajo una Abada a Madrid con un elefante que envió de regalo el gobernador de Java, y dejó perpetuada su memoria, comunicando su nombre a la calle en que estuvo, que hasta hoy llamamos de la Abada.[9]

---

[5] ENTRAMBASAGUAS, *Góngora en Madrid* (Madrid: IEM, 1961), p. 8, and ALONSO, *Góngora y el «Polifemo»,* II, 144-45.

[6] ARTIGAS, p. 65.

[7] JAMMES, *Études sur l'oeuvre poétique de Don Luis de Góngora y Argote* (Bordeaux: IEIIAUB, 1967), p. 116, n. 153. In the same note, Jammes lists two other Góngora sonnets bearing the date 1588 in the Chacón manuscript, «Tengoos, señora tela, gran mancilla» and «Duelete de esa puente, Mançanares», whose attack on the capital city he unconvincingly proposes as a reflection of the same imaginary trip to Madrid. JAMMES notes that Juan Millé y Giménez, *Sobre la génesis del Quijote* (Barcelona: Araluce, 1930), pp. 75-82, believes that Góngora was in Madrid in 1588. This theory is based on Góngora's sonnet «Tu, cuio illustre entre vna i otra almena» addressed to Luis de Vargas, which, according to Millé, was written before 30 March 1588, because Vargas left Toledo before that day to participate in the Spanish Armada. Thus Millé concludes that Góngora, while on the hypothetical trip, must have stopped in Toledo in 1588. ARTIGAS, p. 66, however, suggests that the sonnet was written in 1589 when Góngora, during his trip to Mazuecos, passed through Toledo. See also ENTRAMBASAGUAS, pp. 8-12; he details Góngora's trips to or through Madrid (1589-90, 1592, 1596, 1602, 1609, and 1611 or 1612) in the years before the poet established his residence there in 1617.

[8] See FOULCHÉ-DELBOSC, I, xi and Chapter I, p. 4, in the present study.

[9] LEOPOLDO LUGONES, *Diccionario etimológico del castellano usual* (Buenos Aires: AAL, 1944), p. 36. LUGONES is quoting from Fray Francisco Cañes's *Diccionario español-latino-arábigo* (Madrid: A. Sancha, 1787), I, 2, s.v. «abada». COVARRUBIAS,

The solution to the chronological problem, however, is not as complex as it seems. Góngora went to Madrid in 1589-90, and he had heard about the governor's present to the king, which is mentioned in the first line of his poem and which must have created news in all of the major cities and towns of Spain. Because such magnificent animals were not commonly found in Góngora's homeland, it would make sense that the curious poet went to see the elephant and rhinoceros or that he had at least heard about these imposing beasts, which were most likely still alive only eight years after their arrival in his country.[10] The fame or grandeur of these creatures may have inspired him to write his sonnet, then, around 1590.

That much of Góngora's poetry exists in variants, that there are only minor insignificant textual discrepancies between his other poems in the *cancioneiro* and those in the Chacón manuscript,[11] and that I have established approximate dates for the versions of «Grandes mas que elephantes i que habadas» suggest two possible explanations for «*Cancioneiro*»[12] and its relationship to «Chacón»:

1. Góngora wrote the first version of his sonnet about 1590; this text was included in «*Cancioneiro*» (with some Portuguese modifications) before or in 1610. It is therefore the original of Góngora's poem that he corrected, amended, and considerably improved to produce «Chacón».

2. «Chacón» is the original version of the sonnet. Sometime before 1610, however, it was garbled by a Portuguese-speaking scribe who created another text with semantic, orthographic, and phonological variants.

To better understand the two hypotheses and to explain why I believe the first to be correct, I will turn to the versions themselves. Both «Chacón» and «*Cancioneiro*» mockingly describe the social groups that make up the Court. Góngora, says Juan Antonio Pellicer, «played the part of the waggish stork in Persius: he noted every thing, and pecked at every

pp. 180-81, s.v. «bada», however, confirms the fact that Philip II owned an elephant and a rhinoceros and notes the additional information that they lived for a very long time in the Madrid of Góngora's day: «En nuestros días truxeron al rey Felipe II, que santa gloria aya, una bada, que por mucho tiempo estuvo en Madrid... Y como está dicho arriba, le hemos ya visto en Madrid vivo por muchos días, juntamente con un elefante.» Cf. LUIS DE GÓNGORA, *Sonetos completos*, ed. Biruté Ciplijauskaité (Madrid: Castalia, 1969), p. 157; the MILLÉS, p. 1142, n. 252; and the *Diccionario histórico de la lengua española* (Madrid: RAE, 1933-36), I, 11, s.v. «abada» and II, 12, s.v. «bada».

[10] Members of the elephant family live for approximately 80 years, whereas the different species of rhinoceroses survive until about age 50. See ERNEST P. WALKER, et al., *Mammals of the World* (Baltimore: The Johns Hopkins Press, 1964), II, 1320 and 1349. See also the quotation from Covarrubias in note 9 above.

[11] GÓNGORA's *letrilla*, «Dineros son calidad», and his sonnet, «Iaze debaxo de esta piedra fria» (attributed), contain only a few word variants and spelling changes. Some strophes, in addition, are missing from the *letrilla*; probably they have been repressed or lost by the scribe.

[12] I shall refer to the Chacón text of the sonnet as «Chacón» and to the *cancioneiro* version as «*Cancioneiro*».

29

thing with his satirical pen».[13] More specifically, the poet ridiculed the haughtiness of Spain's grandees, a group who «por su nobleza y mereci-miento tiene en España la preeminencia de poderse cubrir delante del Rey».[14] The grandees were so impressed with themselves that they became overbearing figures, and by Góngora's day, the were earning a well-deserved reputation for stupidity, possibly the result of centuries of in-breeding. Góngora pokes fun at them, in the two versions of the sonnet, by playing on the word «grande» (1) with reference to size, worth (great-ness), and position.

«Abada», found in «Chacón» (1) and *Cancioneiro* (1), means «rhi-noceros»; Joan Corominas traces the word from the Portuguese «bada», commonly employed by Spanish authors of the late sixteenth and early seventeenth centuries.[15] He states, in addition, that the variant «abada» was created by the agglutination of «bada» and its definite article «a», but that it did not appear in Portugal until 1611.[16] The word's inclusion in *Cancionero* and its definition in José Pedro Machado's etymological lexicon, however, suggest that the date supplied by Corominas is too late; the year 1611 must refer to «abada's» dictionary debut:

> Do malaio, *bádaq*, «rinoceronte». Note-se que de início (pràcticamente durante o séc. XVI) esta forma não era a que estava em uso, mas *bada:* «Onde ha outros muytos animaes muyto peyores ainda que aves, como são alifantes, *badas*, liões...», *Pereg.*, cap. 41. Teria sido nos fins da mesma centúria que *abada* começou a correr. A mais ant. abonação que para ela disponho está em texto escrito por volta de 1605... Notar que o primeiro dic. a registrar este voc. foi, como parece, o de Agostinho Barbosa (1611).[17]

The authoritative text of Góngora's sonnet, moreover, reads «habadas». The «h», which writers in the sixteenth and seventeenth centuries seem to have included or omitted at random, is explained by Jerónimo Gómez de Huerta in his translation of Pliny's *Naturalis historia*:

> No se auia visto este animal en Castilla, hasta nuestros tiempos: en los quales truxeron vno presentado al Rey Filipo Segundo, nuestro señor: truxeronle de

---

[13] *Vida de Cervantes*, p. cxiv, apud EDWARD CHURTON, *Góngora* (London: John Murray, 1862), I, 18. Churton cites this book without any bibliographic information, but he is referring to JUAN ANTONIO PELLICER's *Vida de Miguel de Cervantes Saavedra* (Madrid: Gabriel de Sancha, 1800). J. A. Pellicer (1738-1806) is not the commentator of Góngora (José Pellicer, 1602-1679) as the reader might naturally suppose.

[14] *Diccionario de Autoridades*, II, pt. 4, 72, s.v. «grande».

[15] *Diccionario crítico etimológico de la lengua castellana*, I (Madrid: Gredos, 1954), p. 2, s.v. «abada». Corominas further comments: «Por error afirma *Aut[oridades]* que sólo designa la hembra del rinoceronte» (I, 2). There may also be a pun on «abad» (abbot). Góngora would then be poking fun at the powerful ecclesiastics in Madrid.

[16] I, 2, s.v. «abada».

[17] *Dicionário etimológico da língua portuguesa*, 2nd ed. (Lisboa: Confluência, 1967), I, 25, s.v. «abada».

la Fauana, o Habana, isla de los Reynos de Portugal: y assi comunmente la llaman Habada.[18]

Undoubtedly, the silent letter was dropped by writers of the period.[19]

Huerta's interpretation of «(h)abada» was superseded, however, by that of the linguist, Leopoldo de Eguilaz y Yanguas:

> La voz *abada,* cuyo orígen dá Huerta por antojo, es corrupción de wāḥidī, *uahidi* y por transposición del *alef,* síncopa del *hi* medial y conversión de la *i* final en *a, auada ó abada...*[20]

Huerta makes it clear, though, that «habada» or «abada» came from the Portuguese in the late sixteenth century and was adopted by the Spanish people of that time.

Góngora employs «(h)abada» in his dehumanization of imposing grandees, in the first line of the versions, before he extends his satire to include the greed of Madrid's «titulos», men with titles, in lines two and three. To exaggerate the avarice of the nobles, he compares them to «rocas» because such men could not be softened or moved by the needs of others: «para ponderar la avaricia y cortedad de alguno en el dar, se suele decir que es como una roca.»[21] The poet's continued attack on stinginess is commented on by Salcedo Coronel; he points out that the position of *gentilhombre del rey,* although honorable, allowed the aristocrats who served at the king's table to provide for their own mouths and nobody else's:

> ... para motejar de apocados y miserables los Caballeros de Palacio y la Corte, dice sólo son gentiles hombres de su misma boca, significando que no sustenta-ban otra alguna.[22]

---

[18] JERÓNIMO GÓMEZ DE HUERTA, trans., *Historia natural* (Madrid: Luis Sánchez, 1624), I, 387. The statement is from Gómez de Huerta's annotation.

[19] ROBERT K. SPAULDING, *How Spanish Grew* (Berkeley: University of California Press, 1975), p. 89, explains that RAMÓN MENÉNDEZ PIDAL in his *Orígenes del español, RFE,* Anejo No. 1 (Madrid: Hernando, 1926), pp. 238-39, notes that in the year 1578 people in Old Castile said «alagar», but in Toledo people said «halagar». The source of MENÉNDEZ PIDAL's information is Fray Juan de Córdoba's *Arte en lengua zapoteca* (Mexico: Pedro Balli, 1578). Spaulding also comments that, in 1611, COVARRUBIAS, p. 672, s.v. «h», declared that those individuals who did not pronounce the initial consonant of «heno» and «humo» were «pusilánimes, descuidados y de pecho flaco». Thus the «h» was sometimes aspirated and sometimes silent.

[20] *Glosario etimológico de las palabras españolas de origen oriental* (Granada, 1886; rpt. Madrid: Atlas, 1974), p. 6.

[21] DIEGO GARCÍA DE SALCEDO CORONEL, ed., *Segundo tomo de las obras de Don Luis de Góngora* (Madrid: Imprenta Real, 1644), p. 552, apud CIPLIJAUSKAITÉ, *Sonetos completos,* p. 157. Cf. ALONSO, *Góngora y el «Polifemo»,* II, 146.

[22] Apud ALONSO, *Góngora y el «Polifemo»,* II, 146. The nobles, although greedy, were sometimes cash-poor. They had to offer enormous dowries for their daughters, buy gifts for the king, and pay lavish expenses to keep up appearances. Their lands, moreover, were part of entailed estates so that they could not sell any of their property to raise money. See MARCELIN DEFOURNEAUX, *Daily Life in Spain in the Golden Age,* trans. Newton Branch (New York: Praeger, 1971), p. 60: «Certain

Whereas «Chacón's» compact verses demonstrate a variety of poetic techniques as Góngora transforms his impressions of the people and things mentioned in his poem into a caricature of Spain's capital city, the humor in the other text of the sonnet is unsurprisingly expressed with less effectiveness. «Cancioneiro's» variant, «Discrete» [sic] for «Illustri», mitigates the force of Góngora's satire in line four. Mocking the courtiers' tendency to adopt Italian titles, the poet calls these men «Illustri Cauaglier»; they are avid and pretentious officials to the king whose «llaues doradas», keys to wealth, allude to the golden keys that, when fastened to the men's belts, were symbols of their rank.[23] In referring to an aristocrat, «discreto» eliminates Góngora's lighthearted jab at the Spanish nobles' absurd custom of pompously calling themselves by Italian titles.[24] Although it may be intended ironically, «discreto» fails to express enough irony to convey Góngora's scorn, and it praises these courtiers too highly for Góngora's satire: «se dixo discreto, el hombre cuerdo y de buen seso, que sabe ponderar las cosas y dar a cada una su lugar.»[25] Moreover, Damasio de Frías defines discretion as a habit of the intellect, and the discreet person as one who knows how to fit gracefully into any situation at any time in any place.[26] The aristocrats of Spain's Golden Age do not conform to such descriptions. They are, however, illustrious, but not for their discretion; instead, they are conspicuous for their self-importance.

In «Chacón», Góngora incorporates periphrasis into his attack on office seekers: «Habitos, capas digo remendadas» (5). The hábito de Santiago, much coveted by pretenders, had the cross of St. James appliquéd onto it. Appearing patched, «remendada», it was often ridiculed as a sign of poverty or as a lagarto: «Insecto... cuya piel áspera le hace parecer

noblemen, backed by enormous wealth, were able to maintain their high estate at court, despite all the expenditure and 'accessories' entailed. Nevertheless, even the nobility felt the pinch of the general impoverishment of the kingdom.»

[23] «Illustri Cauaglier, llaues doradas», is discussed by Salcedo Coronel in his commentary on Góngora's sonnet, p. 552, apud CIPLIJAUSKAITÉ, Sonetos completos, p. 158 and Sonetos, p. 322.
[24] SALCEDO CORONEL, p. 552, apud ALONSO, Góngora y el «Polifemo», II, 147, notes Góngora's humorous technique: «Para mayor gracejo se valió de este término extranjero ['illustri cavalier'].» «Discreto» is both Italian and Spanish for «discreet» (in Italian it has an accent on the «e»). Thus, the word's impact as an Italian term is lost in the Spanish text.
[25] COVARRUBIAS, p. 475, s.v. «discernir».
[26] See MARGARET J. BATES, «Discreción» in the Works of Cervantes (Washington, D.C.: The Catholic University of America Press, 1945), pp. 74-75 and DAMASIO DE FRÍAS, «Diálogo de la discreción», in Diálogos de diferentes materias inéditos hasta ahora (Madrid: G. Hernández and Galo Sáez, 1929), p. 35 and pp. 83-84. FRÍAS, pp. 75-76, divides the discretos into three groups: the avisados who are discreet in speaking, writing, and dealing with people, the cuerdos who have good judgement and common sense, and the true discretos who have the qualities of both the avisados and the cuerdos. Cf. BATES, p. 77.

manchado... Se llama vulgarmente la insignia del Orden de Santiago.»[27]
Referring to the cloak as a symbol of the mania for seeking an *hábito*,
Góngora's pejorative verse is quite different from the equivalent, but
ordinary line in «*Cancioneiro*» that pointlessly lists the four important
assets of a caballero: «Habitos pleitos cambios embaixadas» (5).

Góngora next aims his skillful rhetoric at the women of the Court.
Whereas «*Cancioneiro's*» variant, «confussa multitud de damas locas» (6),
highlights the crazy personalities of these women, the other version of the
poem presents them from a more precise and somewhat different per-
spective. «*Chacón's*» verse, «Damas de haz i enues, viudas sin tocas» (6),
explains that the women fell into two categories: they were either un-
faithful wives, pretending to be faithful, or widows who, rather than com-
porting themselves properly, aggressively hunted lovers.[28] Góngora's selection of the preposition «sin» indicates that these women, unlike the ladies
and widows of the period, refused to conform to the custom of wearing
mourning mantillas; it emphasizes their masquerade as marriageable spin-
sters.

In the almost identical lines of «*Cancioneiro*» (7-8) and «*Chacón*» (7-8),
Góngora extends his attack on women to include anyone riding around the
city in carriages drawn by beasts: «Carroças de ocho bestias, i aun son
pocas / Con las que tiran i que son tiradas» («Chacón»). Modest wagons
were hitched to two horses and luxury coaches to four; so, in this case,
there are as many animals inside the carriage as outside it. The phrases
«i aun son pocas» («Chacón», 7) and «y son pocas» («*Cancioneiro*», 7),
however, emphasize that, at times, the coaches were overcrowded with
bestial humans[29] who, as the malicious pun on the verb «tirar» implies,
were women of ill repute.[30]

---

[27] The allusion to poverty is made by SALCEDO CORONEL, p. 553, *apud* ALONSO,
Góngora y el «Polifemo», II, 147 and CIPLIJAUSKAITÉ, *Sonetos completos*, p. 158. This
quotation is from the *Diccionario de Autoridades*, II, pt. 4, 351, s.v. «lagarto».

[28] SALCEDO CORONEL, p. 553, *apud* CIPLIJAUSKAITÉ, *Sonetos completos*, p. 158. CIPLI-
JAUSKAITÉ, *Sonetos*, p. 322, mentions Dámaso Alonso's different reading: «D. Alonso
prefiere la lección *dueñas con tocas*; según él, las dueñas eran objeto odioso para
muchos escritores» (*apud* ALONSO, II, 147). Additionally, she refers to a regulation
of admitting women at the Royal Court: «Es curiosa la noticia que da Cabrera...
acerca de un reglamento en la Corte: 'Está mandado que no dejen entrar allí ninguna
cualidad de viudas, aunque tengan negocios... mujeres enamoradas y cortesanas se
permite que entren'» (*apud* LUIS CABRERA DE CÓRDOBA, *Relaciones de las cosas sucedidas en la Corte de España desde 1599 hasta 1614* [Madrid: J. M. Alegría, 1857],
p. 99).

[29] ALONSO, *Góngora y el «Polifemo»*, II, 147, comments on the numbers of animals
and persons.

[30] VÍCTOR LEÓN, *Diccionario de argot español y lenguaje popular*, 2nd ed. (Madrid:
Alianza, 1981), p. 145, s.v. «tirada»: «Puta.» See also LUIS BESSES, *Diccionario de
argot español o lenguaje jergal gitano, delincuente profesional y popular* (Barcelona:
Sucesores de Manuel Soler, 1906), pt. 1, 159, s.v. «tirar». Although the sexual meaning
of «tirar» does not appear in most dictionaries, Basses defines the verb as «fornicar».

The poet's criticism of the Court becomes more scathing, in the first tercet of each version, as he attacks the legal profession. Line nine in «Chacón» is the same in «Cancioneiro»: «Catarriberas, animas en pena.» «Catarriberas» —«falcones»— ironically suggests grasping lawyers and law enforcement officers:

> En la Corte se llaman assí los Abogados que se aplican à salir à pesquisas y otras diligencias semejantes. Y tambien se suele extender a los que se emplean en ser Alcaldes mayores y Corregidores en corregimientos de letras.[31]

These magistrates are «animas en pena» because they spend their time and energy soliciting commissions from their superiors by obsequiously attending to them.[32]

With the assistance of metonymy, «Cancioneiro» captures the meaning of the next verse in the variant, «con Bartolos m'es dada la milicia». «Bartolos», textbooks, is clearly a reference to Bártulo de Sassoferrato, the famous Bolognese jurisconsult of the latter part of the fourteenth century, whose works provided fundamental knowledge for law students. «Con Bartulos i Abbades la milicia», the equivalent verse in «Chacón», alludes to «el Abad Panormitano», another well-known counselor.[33] «Chacón», through two examples of metonymy, is condemning the infighting among officials more emphatically than «Cancioneiro». In both texts, however, the poet criticizes the military as severely as the legal profession because neither organization fulfills its duties: «la milicia operando como corresponde a la jurisprudencia...; y el derecho, en cambio, con violencia y sin justicia.»[34]

Góngora, like all satirists, was probably as concerned with the exposition of his work as with its purpose. Satire enjoys a specific form such as the list, story, or anecdote, whatever the writer finds most appropriate for communicating his point.[35] In «Grandes mas que elephantes i que habadas», Góngora incorporates the technique of pairing items into the list or into the greater scheme of «chaotic enumeration». This term, applied by Biruté Ciplijauskaité to this sonnet, was first employed by Leo Spitzer in reference to modern verse.[36] Góngora, like many twentieth-century poets, uses the technique to convey the pandemonium of the world around him.[37]

---

[31] *Diccionario de Autoridades*, I, pt. 2, 229-30, s.v. «catarribera».
[32] SALCEDO CORONEL, p. 553, *apud* ALONSO, *Góngora y el «Polifemo»*, II, 147.
[33] The definition of «Bartolos» as textbooks is from COROMINAS, I, 417, s.v. «Bártulos». ALONSO, *Góngora y el «Polifemo»*, II, 147, identifies both Bártulo de Sassoferrato and the Abad Panormitano. See also CIPLIJAUSKAITÉ, *Sonetos*, p. 322.
[34] ALONSO, *Góngora y el «Polifemo»*, II, 147.
[35] RONALD PAULSON, *The Fictions of Satire* (Baltimore: The Johns Hopkins University Press, 1967), p. 5, discusses the various forms that an author may employ to convey his satire.
[36] See his *La enumeración caótica en la poesía moderna* (Buenos Aires: Instituto de Filología, 1945).
[37] Other poets of Góngora's day imitated this technique used by the Italians in

Góngora's sonnet even conforms to such «chaotic enumeration» in its conclusion. Commenting on the specifically built court homes, the poet includes, in «Chacón», the phrase «Casas i pechos todo a la malicia» (12). The wealthy noblemen of Madrid who owned houses of more than one floor were obligated to provide lodging for civil servants and other followers of the Court, whereas those who could afford homes of only a single storey were exempt from opening their doors to such strangers. As a result, all aristocrats built one-storey domiciles and the city was heavily populated with these «casas a la malicia», so-called because their small size fraudulently allowed their wealthy owners to escape their responsibilities to the king.[38]

Modeled on «casas a la malicia», «pechos a la malicia», found in «Cancioneiro» (12) and «Chacón» (12), is an expression invented by the poet; it implies that «los pechos», the men's intentions, were also malicious.[39] «Pechos», meaning «taxes», however, is another possible interpretation:

works such as PETRARCH's two sonnets «Grazie ch'a pochi il ciel largo destina» and «Quella fenestra ove l'un sol si vede» and LORENZO DE' MEDICI's «Cerchi chi vuol le pompe e gli alti onori». Góngora's contemporaries also imitated the text of «Grandes mas que elephantes i que habadas». CIPLIJAUSKAITÉ, Sonetos, p. 321, notes that ALONSO (Góngora y el «Polifemo», II, 145-46) believes Villamediana's sonnet about Córdoba and Alessandro Tassoni's composition entitled «Ritratto di Madrid» to be modeled on Góngora's piece, whereas other poets imitated another sonnet, «Una vida bestial de encantamiento», which was attributed to Góngora in the Hoces edition of his poetry. On the same page, Ciplijauskaité adds that the sonnet «Grandes por mil maneras y cuatrocientos», falsely attributed to Villamediana, was based on this questionable poem and that Gustave Lanson claims that Scarron's sonnet against Paris was similarly inspired (see «Études sur les rapports de la littérature française et de la littérature espagnole au XVII° siècle (1600-1660)», RHL, 3 [1896], 327-28). Alonso notes that Francesco Busenello's poem against Madrid was also modeled on «Una vida bestial de encantamiento» (Góngora y el «Polifemo», II, 146; see J. G. FUCILLA, «A Decade of Notes on Spanish Poetry», SP, 32 [1935], 43) and that FRANCISCO MANUEL DE MELO's poem «A vida que fazia em sua prisão» (in spite of its different theme) was dependent on «Grandes mas que elephantes i que habadas». However, Ciplijauskaité (p. 668) remarks that, although «Una vida bestial de encantamiento» is related to «Grandes mas que elephantes i que habadas», its attribution to Góngora has been repudiated by various critics such as José Pellicer, Américo Castro, and D. Alonso. JOSÉ DELEITO Y PIÑUELA, Sólo Madrid es corte (Madrid: Espasa-Calpe, 1942), p. 259, concurs that today the poem is no longer attributed to Góngora. Moreover, the text's inferior quality suggests that it is not likely to be a Góngora precursor to «Grandes mas que elephantes i que habadas», but instead another imitation of this sonnet. In addition, it is noteworthy that the poem includes the words «cambios, embaxadas» (7), which echo «cambios embaixadas» (5) from «Cancioneiro», and the phrase «Esto es Madrid» (14) reminiscent of the first part of «Chacón's» final verse «Esto es la Corte». These observations further suggest that «Una vida bestial de encantamiento» was written after «Grandes mas que elephantes i que habadas»; as Alonso believes (Góngora y el «Polifemo», II, 146), it is most probably an imitation of Góngora's sonnet by an unknown poet.

[38] DELEITO Y PIÑUELA, pp. 23-24. Cf. SALCEDO CORONEL (p. 554) as quoted by CIPLIJAUSKAITÉ, Sonetos completos, p. 158 and Sonetos, p. 322; ALONSO, Góngora y el «Polifemo», II, 148; and BERNARDO ALEMANY Y SELFÁ, Vocabulario de las obras de don Luis de Góngora y Argote (Madrid: RAE, 1930), p. 196, s.v. «casa».

[39] ALONSO, Góngora y el «Polifemo», II, 148 and CIPLIJAUSKAITÉ, Sonetos completos, p. 158.

4

> Redimió después la Villa [Madrid] tan pesado censo [de hospedar a los miem-
> bros de la Corte] con un servicio de 250.000 ducados, equivalente a la sexta
> parte de los alquileres de las casas durante diez años. Pero este tributo pesó
> exclusivamente sobre las construcciones de *más de un piso*.[40]

The hypocritical nobles lived in an environment that Góngora describes with the phrase «Lodos con peregil i ierbabuena» («Chacón», 13). The burlesque metaphor of seasoned mud alludes to the Madrid custom of tossing excrement into the street to the shout of «¡Agua va!»:

> Grave imperfección de la mayoría de las casas era el carecer de retretes. De
> ello se quejaba ya en el siglo XVI el italiano Camilo Borghese (luego Paulo V).
> Años después repetía igual queja Martín Zeilero (o el viajero alemán de quien
> éste tomó sus datos), consignando que, en vez de tan necesarios evacuatorios,
> 'se usan vasijas que, llenas de excrementos, se vacían en calles y plazas, moles-
> tando con su mal olor el olfato de los transeúntes; de cuyo mal se resiente la
> misma villa de Madrid, Corte de tan gran monarquía'.[41]

«Todos» («*Cancioneiro*», 13), however, omits the entire sewer image of the Chacón version. It diminishes Góngora's emphasis on hypocrisy and weakens the impact of «Chacón's» final lines. After lambasting the flaws of society, «Chacón» leaves Madrid to the courtiers: «Esto es la Corte. Buena prò les haga» (14).[42] One can easily deduce that if «*Cancioneiro's*» final verses were substituted for «Chacón's», the sonnet's conclusion would degenerate into an anticlimactic and ineffective one because «dichoso el hombre q̃ de si se escapa» (14)[43] is such a bland understatement.

Clearly, «*Cancioneiro*» is stylistically inferior to «Chacón». It shows occasional copying errors made by its Portuguese-speaking scribe, but its other, more complex, variants that deal with semantics or significantly different lines are too extensive to be dismissed as mere slips of the pen. The anthologist could not have inadvertently created all such variants in a transcription of «Chacón» only because his native language was Portuguese, and it is not likely that he produced them in an effort to improve on «Chacón», a text far superior to «*Cancioneiro*».

The defective piece is best explained as a distorted reflection of an original Góngora version of «Grandes mas que elephantes i que habadas». This earlier text, dated with all probability around 1590 and preserved by

---

[40] DELEITO Y PIÑUELA, p. 23.

[41] DELEITO Y PIÑUELA, pp. 27-28. Cf. JOSÉ LUIS AGUIRRE, *Góngora, su tiempo y su obra; estudio crítico sobre Polifemo* (Madrid: MAS, 1960), p. 71; ALEMANY Y SELFÁ, p. 592, s.v. «lodo»; ALONSO, *Góngora y el «Polifemo»*, II, 148; and SALCEDO CORONEL, p. 554, *apud* CIPLIJAUSKAITÉ, *Sonetos completos*, p. 158 and *Sonetos*, pp. 322-23.

[42] ENTRAMBASAGUAS, p. 5, states that Góngora satirized the new Court (Madrid) «con tal acierto en muchos casos, que sus palabras no s[ó]lo tienen eco en la urbani-zación de la capital de España, bajo el reinado de Carlos III, sino que parecen haber servido de guía en su limpieza y embellecimiento de la época actual».

[43] «Si» is probably an error for «ti» or «aquí».

the garbled copy, was revised by Góngora and became the version presently included in the Chacón manuscript. As noted in Chapter I of this study (p. 4), Foulché-Delbosc, in commenting on Góngora's poetic works, wrote:

> ... puesto que algunas veces [el poeta] corregía o refundía, no es imposible que dos textos distintos de una misma composición sean igualmente auténticos.[44]

The established chronological order (lost text, «Cancioneiro», «Chacón») provides an important insight into Góngora's creative process and into the complex stages through which his work so masterfully proceeded.

Although some versions of Golden Age poems are apocryphal, others are authentic texts or works reflective of original pieces. An analysis of the versions of the sonnet «Grandes mas que elephantes i que habadas» determines the dates of the variant texts and contributes to an understanding of the poetic development of the work. A related study of a Góngora *romance*, Bruce W. Wardropper's critique of the three versions of «La más bella niña», establishes the chronology and authenticity of the ballad's texts.[45] A few versions of Golden Age poems by other authors, such as the variant texts of Quevedo's «Miré los muros de la patria mía»,[46] present similar cases that broaden the reader's comprehension of the poetry of Góngora's day.

B) IMITATION AND CHRONOLOGY IN THE SONNET «MIENTRAS POR COMPETIR CON TU CABELLO»

Some versions of a poem are drafts of one text by the same poet, whereas others are imitations of that text by admirers. A poem or one of its versions, however, may be inspired by the works of different writers. Spanish Renaissance and Baroque poets, when composing verse, were influenced by their Latin and Italian predecessors, in addition to their fellow countrymen. The practice of imitation was respectable in the Golden Age; through it a beginning poet learned everything he could from established poets, either by adopting their style, tone, and attitude, or by making recreations, representations, or plagiarisms of their work.[47] During his apprentice years, Góngora employed Latinisms and other Renaissance commonplaces in his poetry as he imitated the Italian masters.[48] His

---

[44] *Obras poéticas*, I, xiii.

[45] «La más bella niña», *SP*, 63 (1966), 661-62.

[46] See FRANCISCO DE QUEVEDO, *Obra poética*, ed. José M. Blecua (Madrid: Castalia, 1969), I, 184-85, for the versions of the Quevedo poem.

[47] J. A. CUDDON, *A Dictionary of Literary Terms* (New York City: Doubleday, 1977), p. 319.

[48] In *Primera parte de las flores de poetas ilustres de España*, comp. Pedro Espinosa

«Mientras por competir con tu cabello» (1582), generally accepted by modern critics to have been written to outdo Garcilaso's familiar sonnet, «En tanto que de rosa i açucena», is an echo of Ausonius's «Collige, virgo, rosas dum flos novus et nova pubes» and a forerunner of Ronsard's «Quand vous serez bien vieille, au soir, à la chandelle». It is similar to Herrick's later theme, «Gather ye rosebuds while ye may». Alfonso Méndez Plancarte referred to Góngora's poem as a precious variation of carpe diem and of Horace's Odes IV, 10 and 13.[49]

In 1929, J. P. Wickersham Crawford pointed out that Salcedo Coronel and the anonymous commentator of the Primera parte de las flores de poetas ilustres de España had recognized Góngora's acquaintance with Garcilaso's poem.[50] Although Fernando de Herrera believed that Garcilaso, in turn, had imitated Bernardo Tasso's «Mentre che l'aureo crin v'ondeggia intorno», Crawford showed that Góngora's sonnet more closely resembled the phraseology of Tasso's and even suggested an independent use of it.[51] Thirty-one years later, Joseph G. Fucilla, who was less convinced that Góngora was influenced by Tasso, claimed that Góngora's amorous poem was only remotely related to Tasso's and had very little in common with another accepted source, Petrarch's «La testa or fino et calda neve il volto».[52]

The similarity between Garcilaso's and Góngora's sonnets, the clear chronology of the two poems, and Góngora's familiarity with his predecessor's work suggest that Góngora was influenced by Garcilaso's sonnet that follows:

> En tanto que de rosa i açucena
> se muestra la color en vuestro gesto,
> i que vuestro mirar ardiente, onesto
> enciende al coraçon i lo refrena;
> 5 I en tanto qu' el cabello, qu' en la vena
> del oro s'escogio, con buelo presto
> por el hermoso cuello, blanco, enhiesto

(Valladolid: Luis Sánchez, 1605), 2nd ed., ed. Juan Quirós de los Ríos and Francisco Rodríguez Marín (Sevilla: E. Rasco, 1896), p. 381, for example, the anonymous commentator notes that Góngora's seventeenth-century annotator Salcedo Coronel and the eighteenth- and nineteenth-century critic Bartolomé José Gallardo considered Góngora's sonnet «Illustre i hermossissima Maria» to be an imitation of Garcilaso's «En tanto que de rosa i açucena». The anonymous commentator further points out that Salcedo Coronel observed the similarity between these two poems and Góngora's «Mientras por competir con tu cabello» (p. 405).

[49] Cuestiúnculas gongorinas (Mexico: Andrea, 1955), p. 36.

[50] «Italian Sources of Góngora's Poetry», RR, 20 (1929), 126.

[51] CRAWFORD, p. 126. See CIPLIJAUSKAITÉ, Sonetos, p. 440, who mentions Crawford and who, pp. 439-42, cites all manuscript and printed versions of Góngora's sonnet and a comprehensive catalogue of textual variants.

[52] «Góngora», in Estudios sobre el petrarquismo en España, RFE, Anejo No. 72 (Madrid: CSIC, 1960), p. 254.

el viento mueve, esparze i desordena;
Coged de vuestra alegre primavera
10   el dulce fruto, antes q̄ el tiempo airado
cubra de nieve la hermosa cumbre.
Marchitarà la rosa el viento elado,
todo lo mudarà la edad ligera,
por no hazer mudança en su costumbre.[53]

The dignified sobriety of this poem, however, contrasts with the feeling of exhuberance and seduction emitted by Góngora's verses describing feminine beauty.[54] In his purely Renaissance text, Garcilaso equates nature's beauty with that of womankind; the lady in his sonnet has a rosy and lily-white complexion and hair as yellow as gold.

For Góngora, «cabello» (1) is not simply compared to, but is superior to «oro bruñido» (2), «blanca frente» (4) to «lilio bello» (4), «cuello» (8) to «crystal» (8), and «labio» (5) to «clauel» (6):

Mientras por competir con tu cabello,
Oro bruñido al Sol relumbra en vano,
Mientras con menosprecio en medio el llano
Mira tu blanca frente el lilio bello;
5 Mientras a cada labio, por cogello,
Siguen mas ojos que al clauel temprano,
I mientras triumpha con desden loçano
De el luciente crystal tu gentil cuello;
Goça cuello, cabello, labio, i frente,
10 Antes que lo que fue en tu edad dorada
Oro, lilio, clauel, crystal luciente,
No solo en plata o viola troncada
Se vuelua, mas tu i ello juntamente
En tierra, en humo, en poluo, en sombra, en nada.

(CHACÓN: FOULCHÉ-DELBOSC, I, 29-30)[55]

[53] GARCILASO DE LA VEGA, *Obras con anotaciones de Fernando de Herrera* (Sevilla: Alonso de la Barrera, 1580), facs., ed. Antonio Gallego Morell (Madrid: CSIC, 1973), p. 174.

[54] RAFAEL LAPESA, «Sobre algunos sonetos de Garcilaso», in *La poesía de Garcilaso*, ed. Elias L. Rivers (Barcelona: Ariel, 1974), pp. 99-100, states that Garcilaso's interpretation of *carpe diem* «no muestra el alocado júbilo de Lorenzo el Magnífico, la gracia despreocupada de Bernardo Tasso ni la vivaz galantería de Ronsard; se distingue, en cambio, por un sello de dignidad que da elegancia al epicureísmo. Como el mirar de la doncella, 'ardiente', 'honesto', el soneto garcilasiano 'enciende el corazón y lo refrena'».

[55] My translation of Góngora's «Mientras por competir con tu cabello» appears here: While, to compete with your hair, sunlight on polished gold shines in vain; while, in the midst of the plain, your white forehead looks scornfully at the beautiful lily; while more eyes follow each lip to kiss it than pursue the early carnation to pluck it; and while, with bold disdain, your elegant neck triumphs over glistening crystal; enjoy neck, hair, lip, and forehead, before that which was in your prime gold, lily, carnation, shining crystal, not only turns into silver or a truncated violet, but you and all your attributes together into earth, smoke, dust, shadow, nothingness.

The poet first employs metaphors about nature to exalt the lady's beauty. Next, he figuratively destroys her physical assets by likening them to death and decay rather than to nature's splendor. Góngora's poetic art, then, is a representation and elaboration of nature that he carries to extremes.

In 1605, «Mientras por competir con tu cabello» was published, with its tercets altered, in Andrés Rey de Artieda's *Discursos, epístolas y epigramas de Artimidoro* (Zaragoza) under the name of Antonio Vázquez, an unknown soldier-poet.[56] The approbation of this collection is dated 14 October 1604,[57] but Vázquez's poem (first printed in this miscellany) may have been circulating in manuscript form for several years before that date. Because the chronology of Góngora's and Vázquez's sonnets is uncertain, it is difficult to ascertain whether Vázquez imitated Góngora or whether Góngora borrowed from him. But, as indicated by Ciplijauskaité, in her 1969 edition of Góngora's sonnets, critics assume that Góngora's tercets were «alterados» by the hack poet Vázquez (p. 222). José M. Cossío, in his «De bibliografía gongorina», comments that Vázquez's poem «más parece reconstrucción del espléndido soneto de D. Luis, hecha por quien mal lo recordaba, o versión primitiva de él sometida luego a feliz depuración».[58] Cossío adds that the written tradition of Góngora's poetry may account for the variant text but that Rey de Artieda's attribution of the poem to Vázquez is inexplicable, unless the compiler was ignorant of Góngora's sonnet and Vázquez plagiarized Góngora's work (p. 65).[59]

An analysis of the poems, however, sheds new light on the problems of chronology and imitation, often difficulties in dealing with Góngora's texts. Vázquez's poem, which begins with the same introductory verse as Góngora's, is significantly different in technique and theme:

Del Sargento mayor, Antonio Vazquez, a
la edad que passa.

Mientras por competir con tu cabello
relumbra el oro de la Arabia en vano
y mientras conuencido en medio el llano
mira tu blanca frente, el lirio bello,
5   Mientras a cada labio por cojello,
siguen mas ojos que a clauel temprano
mientras tu hermosa, larga y blanca mano
en competencia da parias al cuello.
Goza cabello, cuello, labio, y frente,

[56] CIPLIJAUSKAITÉ, *Sonetos completos*, p. 222 and *Sonetos*, p. 441. Cf. FOULCHÉ-DELBOSC, *Obras poéticas*, III, 92 and 114, who also notes that this sonnet was published in 1605 in Rey de Artieda's collection.
[57] RAYMOND FOULCHÉ-DELBOSC, «Bibliographie de Góngora», *RHi*, 18 (1908), 85.
[58] *RFE*, 19 (1932), 64.
[59] Cf. CIPLIJAUSKAITÉ, *Sonetos*, p. 441, who states that Cossío believed Vázquez's poem to be «un plagio consciente».

10   antes que el tiempo te resuelua en nada,
      lo diafano, claro y transparente.
        Porque la flor de juuentud passada,
      el que alabare la vejez, o miente,
      o es falto de juyzio, si le agrada.

(FOULCHÉ-DELBOSC, «Bibliographie», p. 85)

Vázquez's sonnet lacks the impact of Góngora's metaphoric exaggeration because his verse, «relumbra el oro de la Arabia en vano» (2), is a weak comparison to Góngora's hyperbole, «Oro bruñido al Sol relumbra en vano» (2).[60] The sun that tries in perfect reflecting conditions to compete with the brightness of the woman's golden hair is reduced to the luster of Arabian gold. Whereas the two images exalt woman's beauty over that of nature, only Góngora's metaphor modifies and elevates it to the divine level. Acting as less of a Renaissance commonplace than the sun, the lily in Vázquez's sonnet (3-4) admits to being outdone by the lady's alabaster complexion. The same flower in Góngora's version (3-4) hardly compares to Garcilaso's *azucena* as it is scorned by the lady's white brow.

The poetic *topos* that nature surpasses artistic beauty is paralleled in Góngora's description of the lady's natural beauty; her neck is more elegant than the crystal stem of a wine glass (7-8). Vázquez, however, merely echoes Garcilaso by equating the woman's beauty to that of nature (7-8). Moreover, in choosing her own long white hand as the rival of her neck, his observation is that feminine pulchritude competes with feminine pulchritude, a poetic tautology.

The common pretended or invented elements composing metaphor assert that one thing is another when in reality it is not.[61] In Góngora's poetic world of concrete illusions, the woman's neck almost becomes the object it is modeling or a conversion may be said to have taken place.[62] Góngora the metaphysician, by not exactly equating her neck with the glass stem, causes the woman's physical traits to attain a quasi-abstract and elusive quality not achieved in Vázquez's sonnet.

Hoping to cause the lady to turn her attentions to him, Góngora threatens her with the shocking truth that her loveliness, which transcends that of art and nature, will soon fade; her golden hair will turn to «plata»,

[60] ALFREDO CARBALLO PICAZO, «El soneto 'Mientras por competir con tu cabello', de Góngora», *RFE*, 47 (1964), 379-80, points out that «al» has the variant «el». Either reading serves Góngora's purpose. If «el» is correct, it is the sun that competes in vain with the golden hair; if «al» is correct, it is the sunlight on gold that shines to the hair in vain.

[61] HEINRICH HENEL, «Metaphor and Meaning», in *The Disciplines of Criticism*, ed. Peter Demetz, Thomas Greene, and Lowry Nelson (New Haven: Yale University Press, 1968), p. 114.

[62] Cf. COLIN MURRAY TURBAYNE, *The Myth of Metaphor* (New Haven: Yale University Press, 1962), p. 24. Turbayne uses the word «confusion» to describe a «conversion».

her elegant neck will become a «viola troncada», and all of her physical attributes will decompose into «tierra», «humo», «poluo», «sombra», and «nada» (12-14). Góngora is aware his metaphoric illusion will not endure and he demonstrates that, because the world of artifice is incapable of figuratively taking over the real world for very long, all illusions are transitory and perishable.[63] Vázquez, who fails to produce the *energeia*[64] necessary to create a poetic illusion, can only warn that feminine beauty will become nothingness before he proceeds to make a platitudinous comment on old age (12-14). The previous allusion to death and decay has been glossed over by the poet's sententious statement about growing old. He has thereby mitigated the strength of the first ten lines of his sonnet.

Whereas Garcilaso and Vázquez were mostly concerned with love or feminine beauty, Góngora was preoccupied with human existence as the final lines of «Mientras por competir con tu cabello» cry out in horror at the thought of death, even though they employ feminine beauty as the vehicle for such an expression.[65] Because Vázquez's poem is so obviously inferior to Góngora's, it is hard to imagine why he would have tampered with the master's text and why he would have restored Garcilaso's focal point, old age. This conclusion and the uncertain chronology of the poems strongly suggest that Vázquez was influenced by Garcilaso and that Góngora imitated Vázquez.[66]

The issues of imitation and chronology regarding «Mientras por competir con tu cabello» are further complicated by another version of the poem, which appears under Góngora's name in a rare book entitled *Varias descripciones del tiempo, y de las estaciones del año*, compiled by Josef de Valdivieso[67] (José de Valdivielso, 1560-1638). Entrambasaguas, in his

---

[63] FRANK J. WARNKE, *Versions of Baroque* (New Haven: Yale University Press, 1972), p. 102: «Góngora's hyperboles express the obsessive Baroque concern with the illusoriness of the phenomenal and the transitoriness of all earthly experiences.»

[64] JEAN HAGSTRUM, *The Sister Arts* (Chicago: University of Chicago Press, 1958), p. 12, explains that *energeia*, a term of Greek origin adopted by Aristotle, «refers to the actualization of potency, the realization of capacity or capability, the achievement in art and rhetoric of the dynamic and purposive life of nature». Hagstrum notes that *energeia* is a little different from *enargeia*, used by Plutarch and Horace, which «implies the achievement in verbal discourse of a natural quality or of a pictorial quality that is highly natural».

[65] DÁMASO ALONSO, *Góngora y el «Polifemo»*, II, 134, *apud* CARBALLO PICAZO, p. 398: «Lo impresionante en este soneto de Góngora es el final: toda la imaginería colorista se derrumba y aniquila en ese verso último. El violento contraste barroco asoma ya en esta obra maestra juvenil.»

[66] It is possible that Vázquez's sonnet may have been the product of an academic contest to rewrite Góngora's famous poem, a type of parlor game common in Góngora's day. This idea is merely conjecture, however, and most likely dubious because only one rather poorly written sonnet, Vázquez's poem, would appear to have survived the contest.

[67] (Palma: Felipe Guasp, 1817).

42

Estudios y ensayos sobre Góngora y el barroco,[68] also reproduces this version (p. 71), but the following text is cited from the rare collection:

> Mientras que refulgente tu cabello,
> oro bruñido al sol supera ufano;
> mientras que con desprecio en campo llano
> tu blanca frente afrenta al lirio bello:
> 5 Mientras que cada labio es un destello,
> que luz despide, qual clavel temprano,
> y mientras triunfa con desden lozano,
> del luciente marfil tu gentil cuello:
> Si al ver cuello, cabello, labio y frente,
> 10 asi presumes ser engalanada,
> oro, lirio, clavel, marfil luciente;
> Considera que al fin de tu jornada,
> todo esto ha de parar seguramente,
> en humo, tierra, polvo, sombra, y nada.
>
> (pp. 27-28)

Although the anthology was published in 1817 (and perhaps there were earlier editions), the poem, which was collected by the compiler who died in 1638, undoubtedly came from some sixteenth- or seventeenth-century manuscript. The frontispiece of the book states that the poems included therein were «nuevamente coordinadas y corregidas», and Entrambasaguas comments on the work's introductory note:

> ... lleva una *Nota* anónima al comienzo (págs. 3-4) sin interés a lo que nos importa, porque no indica nada respecto de corrección del texto de Góngora...
> (*Estudios,* p. 71)

The first six lines of the sonnet in Valdivielso's anthology differ in part from those of the Chacón version. In the Valdivielso text, the sun does not compete in vain with the luster of the woman's hair as in the Chacón version (1-2), but instead the refulgence of the lady's golden locks haughtily surpasses the radiance of the sun (1-2). Likewise her brow, which scorns the lily in the Chacón text (3-4), insults that flower's whiteness in the Valdivielso version (3-4). Whereas the lips of the lady in the authoritative poem draw more attention than the first carnation of spring (5-6), the lips of the woman in the other text are as scintillating as that early blossom (5-6). The variants in the two quatrains of the Valdivielso version consist of words more powerful in meaning than those in the Chacón text. Such terminology —«refulgente» (1), «supera ufano» (2), «desprecio» (3), «afrenta» (4), «destello» (5), «luz despide» (6)— is more in keeping with the forceful conclusion of Góngora's authoritative poem than with that of the Valdivielso version, which ends less emphatically. It is at this point

---

[68] (Madrid: Nacional, 1975).

in the sonnet, after lines seven and eight (which are the same in both versions), that the Valdivielso text becomes decidedly inferior to that of the Chacón manuscript. Whereas Góngora commands the lady to enjoy her youthful beauty before it fades into nothingness, in the Valdivielso text the lady is admonished that, although she may presume herself to be lovely now, she should not forget her mortality, because her travels through life along with all of her beauty will eventually reach their conclusion. The image of life as a journey that terminates in nothingness maintains Góngora's Baroque focal point about the horror of death but weakens the impact of the poem's final tercet. Moreover, the last line of the Valdivielso version, which describes life or the journey as ending «en humo, tierra, polvo, sombra, y nada», has a problem with its word order. The lady will die and her body decompose, not first into «humo» and then into «tierra», but rather into «tierra, humo, polvo, sombra, y nada».

The Valdivielso version clearly has its flaws. Entrambasaguas reproduces it without making any statements about its significance. The text, published under Góngora's name, could be an intermediate version by Góngora that he later revised to produce the Chacón poem. It is also possible, however, that the Valdivielso version may have been modified by a creative scribe, amended by Valdivielso, or perhaps corrected by a nineteenth-century editor.[69] Even though the note at the beginning of the anthology mentions no revisions of Góngora's poem or of any other poems, except for Valdivielso's, this version may have been altered in the sixteenth or seventeenth centuries, either before it became a part of Valdivielso's collection or when Valdivielso included it in his anthology. Another theory is that a nineteenth-century editor may have altered it preceding its publication in 1817. The Valdivielso version, in addition, more closely resembles the Chacón text than that of Vázquez. The Chacón version includes lines similar or identical to those of Vázquez's poem, and the Valdivielso text, in turn, has verses that echo or are identical to those of the Chacón piece. Furthermore, the Valdivielso version has no lines that are the same as any of those in Váquez's text, and the verses in the Valdivielso sonnet that resemble lines of Vázquez's poem are also similar to the corresponding verses of the Chacón text to an equal or greater degree. Thus, it appears that the correct chronological order of the sonnets is Vázquez, Chacón, Valdivielso. The high quality of the Valdivielso version's quatrains, the inferior quality of its tercets, all that it has in common with the Chacón text, and the little that it shares with the Vázquez poem strongly suggest it is a corruption of the Chacón version. I believe, then, that Vázquez was inspired by Garcilaso and imitated by Góngora and that Góngora was

---

[69] It is not clear if the poems in the anthology were «Nuevamente coordinadas y corregidas» by Valdivielso or by someone else before their publication in 1817.

copied by a creative scribe or anthologist who produced the text printed in the Valdivielso collection.

C) THE SONNET «O CLARO HONOR DEL LIQUIDO ELEMENTO» AS IMITATED IMITATION

Góngora has been recognized as the imitator of other poets' verse,[70] but his contemporaries and successors have also imitated his work, creating similar versions of his texts. The sonnet «O claro honor del liquido elemento» (1582) is an example of a poem by Góngora that was modeled on the verse of a predecessor, in this case, Bernardo Tasso's «Ó puro, ó dolce, ó fiumicel de argento».[71] Góngora's poem was in turn imitated by don Miguel Antonio Caro,[72] who wrote a sonnet entitled «A una fuente». Caro's text, which begins with the same first line as Góngora's, was published in *Las Provincias,* a Valencian newspaper, on 16 December 1893.[73] The three sonnets appear as follows in chronological order:

Ó puro, ó dolce, ó fiumicel de argento
Piu ricco assai, c'Hermo, Pattolo, ó Tago,
Che vai al tuo camin lucente è vago
Fra le sponde di gemme à passo lento.
5   Ó primo onor del liquido elemento,
Conserva integra quella bella imago,
Di cui non pur quest' occhi infermi appago
Ma pasco di dolc' esca il mio tormento.
    Qual hora in te si specchia, è nelle chiare
10   E lucid' onde tue, si lava il volto
Colei, ch' arder potrebbe orsi, è serpenti:
    Ferma il tuo corso, e tutto in te raccolto
Condensa i liquor tuoi caldi è ardenti
Per non portar tanta richeza al mare.

(B. TASSO: *Primera parte de las flores,* p. 347)

O claro honor del liquido elemento,
Dulce arroiuelo de corriente plata

---

[70] See *Primera parte de las flores,* p. 381. The anonymous commentator points out that Salcedo Coronel believed some of Góngora's sonnets to be imitations of Italian poems.

[71] See SALCEDO CORONEL, II, 380, *apud* the anonymous commentator, *Primera parte de las flores,* p. 346. Góngora's sonnet is found in the Chacón manuscript, FOULCHÉ-DELBOSC, I, 25. Góngora's and Tasso's poems appear in the *Primera parte de las flores,* pp. 52 and 347, respectively. Tasso's poem was written in or before 1534 as it is published in his *Rime di Bernardo Tasso* (Vinegia: Ioan. Ant. da Sabio, 1534). See also CIPLIJAUSKAITÉ, *Sonetos,* pp. 228-29, who notes all manuscript and printed versions of Góngora's poem and all textual variants.

[72] Caro was a Columbian writer, humanist, and past president of his country (1894-98). His poem is reproduced in the *Primera parte de las flores,* p. 346.

[73] *Primera parte de las flores,* p. 346.

45

Cuia agua entre la ierua se dilata
Con regalado son, con passo lento;
5 Pues la por quien elar i arder me siento
(Mientras en ti se mira), Amor retrata
De su rostro la nieue i la escarlata
En tu tranquilo i blando mouimiento,
Vete como te vas; no dexes floxa
10 La vndosa rienda al crystalino freno
Con que gouiernas tu veloz corriente;
Que no es bien que confusamente acoja
Tanta belleça en su profundo seno
El gran Señor dèl humido tridente.

(CHACÓN: FOULCHÉ-DELBOSC, I, 25)[74]

¡Oh claro honor del líquido elemento,
Dulce arroyuelo de luciente plata,
Cuya agua entre la hierba se dilata
Con regalado són, con paso lento!
5 Pues aquella hermosura, monumento
De celeste favor, que el mundo acata,
En tu seno se mira, y fiel retrata
Tu límpido cristal tan gran portento,
No borres, al correr, la imagen bella,
10 Que descuido sacrílego sería;
Manso llévala al mar envuelta en flores;
Y el mar, al recibirla, admire en ella
La belleza mayor que el suelo cría,
Y en templos de coral le rinda honores.

(CARO: *Primera parte de las flores*, p. 346)

In both Tasso's and Góngora's poems a clear brook reflects the image
of a beautiful lady as she admires herself in its waters. Tasso asks the creek
in his text to stop its course so that the lady's image, which enriches the
stream, will not flow away from him and out to sea. Similarly, in his
verses, Góngora orders the brook to proceed less swiftly so that the lady's
image, which the stream is transporting to Neptune, will arrive intact for
the god of the ocean to guard in his fluid depths.[75]

---

[74] Góngora's «O claro honor del liquido elemento» translates as follows: Oh clear
honor of the liquid element, sweet little brook of running silver, the water of which
flows amidst the grass with a delicate sound, with a slow gait, since, in your tranquil
and smooth movement, Love portrays the snow and the scarlet of her face, for whom
I feel myself burn and freeze (while she looks at herself in you), continue along as
you are flowing; do not leave slack the wavy rein of the crystalline bridle with
which you regulate your swift current, because it is not fitting that the great god of
the humid trident receive confusedly so much beauty into his profound bay.

[75] Sir RICHARD FANSHAWE, *Shorter Poems and Translations*, ed. N. W. Bawcutt
(Liverpool: Liverpool University Press, 1964), p. 34, loosely translates the final three
lines of Góngora's sonnet as follows: «For it is not fit / Neptune with all the treasures
he doth hold / Should so much beauty in his Armes infold.» JAMMES, *Études*, p. 367,
who does not concur with Fanshawe's translation of Góngora's second tercet, offers a
more plausible interpretation: «... alors que Bernardo Tasso demandait au ruisseau

Caro's poem has the same first strophe as Góngora's except for a one-word variant. Whereas Góngora describes his brook as «corriente plata» (2), Caro refers to his fountain as «luciente plata» (2). «Luciente» emphasizes the glossy quality of both water and «plata», but «corriente» suggests the swift movement of the creek, comparing this stream to liquid metal. Because silver must be heated to a very high temperature to melt, the cool waters normally found in a brook are contrasted with those now hot with the poet's desire.

Although the beginning lines of the two poems are almost identical, the remaining ten verses are significantly different. In Góngora's sonnet, the poet's heart simultaneously burns and freezes out of love for the lady he adores. She incites and restrains his desires —an antithesis commonly found in Renaissance poetry and particularly reminiscent of Garcilaso's verses «i que vuestro mirar ardiente, onesto / enciende al coraçon i lo refrena» (3-4) from the sonnet «En tanto que de rosa i açucena».[76] The woman in Góngora's text who affects the poet in this way looks at herself in the stream where Love has copied «la nieue i la escarlata» (7); the reflection of her face with its white skin and rosy cheeks is seen in the gently and tranquilly moving waters that carry her image seaward. Earthly beauty, represented by the beloved, is portrayed by Love and immortalized by the creek —a symbol of eternity. In Caro's revision of Góngora's poem, divine beauty, suggestive of a lady, the heavens, or the fountain to which the sonnet is directed, is imitated by the fountain's pool. The celestial beauty, a worldly monument of ethereal favor, is depicted in the clear spring; the crystal (water) faithfully imitates (reflects) the great wonder (the lady, the heavens, or the fountain itself).

Góngora, in his sonnet, urges the brook to continue to flow slowly into the ocean by not loosening the wavy rein of its crystalline bridle that controls the swift current. The poet wants the stream to move less rapidly because he believes that Neptune should not receive a confused image of the lady's beauty into his aqueous depths. Caro's imitation is similar to Góngora's text in that Caro orders the spring not to erase the celestial image of beauty by flowing too fast because such an act would be a careless sacrilege. Instead, he commands the fountain's waters to transport the image, surrounded by flowers, into the open ocean. On receiving it, the sea admires the heavenly pulchritude that, although divine, the earth has created, and the briny deep honors this wondrous beauty by displaying it in temples of coral. Likewise, Góngora honors Tasso's poem and Caro

d'arrêter son cours pour ne pas livrer l'image et le souvenir de sa dame à la mer, Góngora veut seulement qu'il modère ses vagues, pour conserver intacte l'image qu'il portera jusqu'à Neptune.»

[76] See GARCILASO's text in his *Obras*, p. 174 and in Chapter III, pp. 38-39 of the present study.

Góngora's, each by imitating the verse of his predecessor in his own sonnet.

Similar poems may be versions of one text by the same author or versions of one text produced by creative scribes or anthologists who chose to edit or alter a given work. Such pieces may also be imitations by poets who tried either to match the verse of a more experienced and admired predecessor or to improve on a text that inspired them. Imitators often made recreations or representations of established poems. Whereas some versions were merely plagiarisms, others were reproductions of an author's style, tone, and attitude composed by amateurs who hoped to learn the art of writing poetry from their mentors. Góngora emulated the work of his predecessors, and his verse was imitated by his contemporaries and successors. The resulting imitations and versions of Góngora's texts are an important contribution to the history of his poetry and to that of the Spanish Golden Age.

IV

DIVERSE VERSIONS

«Trepan los gitanos»: Imitation, Source,
   or Earlier Góngora Work

Caro's poem «A una fuente» is clearly an imitation of Góngora's sonnet «O claro honor del liquido elemento». However, a so-called anonymous imitation of a text may turn out to be either a source of that text or a different version of it by the same poet. Thus, the question of imitation, dependent on the issues of authorship and chronology, is sometimes difficult to determine. The complexity of this question is illustrated by Góngora's *romancillo*,[1] «Trepan los Gitanos», which exists in three versions: one in the Chacón manuscript,[2] one in the Hoces anthology (fol. 103r-v), and one published anonymously in the *Segunda parte del Romancero general y flor de diversa poesía* compiled by Miguel de Madrigal.[3] «Chacón» and «Hoces», both by Góngora, are essentially the same except that «Hoces» suppresses «Chacón's» final strophe.[4] The Chacón and Hoces versions differ radically from the Madrigal text, which is an entirely new poem based on the same *villancico* as the other two versions. «Chacón» consists of seven strophes, each composed of eighteen lines, whereas «Madrigal» contains only three

[1] Although similar to a *letrilla*, the poem is technically a *romancillo*. Note that except for the refrain, each verse scans six syllables, and that assonance in é-a is sustained throughout the poem. The Millés include it under *ROMANCES,* Hoces lists it beneath the heading *ROMANCES BURLESCOS,* Vicuña prints it under *ROMAN-CES SATÍRICOS,* and Jammes does not include it in his *Letrillas.* Its exaggerated musical quality, dancelike movement, refrain, and *cabeza,* however, characterize it as a *letrilla.*

[2] See Foulché-Delbosc, I, 260-64.

[3] (Valladolid: Antonio García, 1605), facs. ed. Joaquín de Entrambasaguas (Madrid: CSIC, 1948), II, 50-51. The Madrigal version of «Trepan los Gitanos» is also included in González Palencia's edition of the *Romancero general 1600, 1604, 1605,* II, 322. Moreover, González Palencia reproduces the Madrigal collection (including its original frontispiece with the publication data: Valladolid: Antonio García, 1605) in the second volume of his edition (pp. 205-358).

[4] I shall refer to the three versions of «Trepan los Gitanos» as «Chacón», «Hoces», and «Madrigal». Because the Hoces and Chacón texts are basically the same, I shall reproduce only the Chacón version.

strophes, each of which is fourteen lines long. None of the strophes printed in «Madrigal» are identical to any of those included in «Chacón» or «Hoces». At best, a few scattered lines in «Madrigal» resemble those in the Chacón and Hoces versions; yet the execution of the themes of deception and money strongly parallel each other in all three texts:

<blockquote>

Trepan los Gitanos
  I bailan ellas,
Otro nudo a la bolsa
  Mientras que trepan.

5 Gitanos de Corte,
Que sobre su rueda
Les mostrò Fortuna
A dar muchas bueltas.
Si en vn costal otros
10 Han dado cient trepas,
En vn çurron estos
Daràn quatrocientas.
Desuanecen hombres,
Mas quien ai que pueda
15 Viendo andar de manos
No dar de cabeça?
I si vnos dan brincos
De rubies, i perlas,
Otros como locos
20 Tiran estas piedras.
Otro nudo a la bolsa
  Mientras que trepan.

Canta en vuestra esquina
Vna cancion tierna
25 El page con plumas,
Paxaro sin ellas,
Blando ruiseñor,
Que en noche serena
Dulce os adormece,
30 I dulce os recuerda.
Si su amo, en tanto,
Por hierros de rexa,
Que os suspende el quiebro,
La hija os requiebra,
35 Dèste ruiseñor
Os guardad, que os echa
Como alano al page,
Que os asga la oreja.
Otro nudo a la bolsa
40 Mientras que trepan.

A vos canta el page,
Buen viejo, que a ella
Letrillas de cambio
Le cantan terceras:

</blockquote>

45   Que no ai pie de copla
       De ningun Póèta
       Como los de vn banco,
       I mas si no quiebra.
       No os fies dèl quicio,
50   Requerid la puerta,
       Que dada la vncion,
       Sin habla os espera.
       Baxad, si por dicha
       No quereis que, mientras
55   Forma el page puntos,
       Meta el amo letra.
       Otro nudo a la bolsa
         Mientras que trepan.

       En Valladolid
60   No ay Gitana bella
       Que no haga mudanças
       Estandose queda.
       El pie sobre corcho
       (Mirad que firmeza)
65   Mueue con buen aire
       Mi honra, i la vuestra.
       Al son de vn pandero,
       Que a su gusto suena,
       Deshaze cruzados,
70   Que es buena moneda.
       I al Conde mas rico,
       Que bayla con ella,
       Conde de Gitanos,
       Desnudo le dexa.
75   Otro nudo a la bolsa
         Mientras que trepan.

       Miran de la mano
       La palma que lleua
       Datiles de oro,
80   La que no, no es buena.
       De las vidas hazen
       Cabes de a paleta,
       Que passan las raias
       Hasta las muñecas.
85   Estrellas os hallan,
       Que mugeres dèstas
       En medio dèl dia
       Hazen ver estrellas.
       Buscan os el aspa,
90   Mas, segun dan bueltas,
       Antes hallaràn
       Las deuanaderas.
       Otro nudo a la bolsa
         Mientras que trepan.

5

95 Sobre quatro palmos
De vna vara estrecha
Haze el mercader
Cient mil ligerezas.
Buela por el mundo
100 La pluma en la oreja
Dando estraños saltos
De vna en otra feria,
Sin temer caìda,
Porque sobre seda
105 Caìdas de gato
Nunca dieron pena.
Fardos de Logroño
Se cargan apriessa,
Que para trepar
110 Se escombra la tienda.
Otro nudo a la bolsa
   Mientras que trepan.

Ay otros Gitanos
De mejor conciencia,
115 Saludables de vñas,
Sin ser grandes bestias,
Maestros famosos
De hazer barrenas,
Que taladran almas,
120 Por clauar haziendas;
Para cuio fin
Humildes menéàn
De la passion santa
La santa herramienta,
125 Clauos, i tenaças,
I para ascendencia
De años a esta parte
La santa escalera.
Otro nudo a la bolsa
130 Mientras que trepan.

(CHACÓN: FOULCHÉ-DELBOSC, I, 260-64)[5]

---

[5] The gypsy boys steal and the gypsy girls dance. Put another knot in your purse while they go around stealing. Fortune showed the gypsies of this town, who had their hands on her wheel, how to give it many turns. If, in a large cloth sack, others have committed a hundred frauds, in a large fur bag, these gypsies will commit four hundred. Men lose their strength, but who is there who can steal seeing that he not lose his own fortune? And, if some give away valuable trinkets of rubies and pearls, others, like crazy men, throw away these stones. Put another knot in your purse while they go around stealing. He sings on your corner a tender song, the page with feathers, like a bird without them, the gentle nightingale that in the serene night sweetly lulls you to sleep and sweetly remembers you. Although his master, in the meantime, through iron grates, frees you from harm, courts your daughter; be careful of this nightingale who throws you like a mastiff to the page so he can grasp your ear. Put another knot in your purse while they go around stealing. The page sings to you, good old man, for procuresses sing their bills of exchange to her, because there is no

Letra.

Trepan los Gitanos,
y baylan ellas,
otro nudo a la bolsa
mientras que trepan.

5   Gitanos del mundo,
que suelen dar bueltas
por quitar a vezes
otras de cadena.
Cuyas coyunturas,
10   para no perderlas,
si son de hurtar,
se doblan y quiebran.
Pues que de ligeros
muchas vezes buelan,
15   como Aguilas Reales,
de las faldriqueras,
otro nudo a la bolsa
mientras que trepan.

Cantores con passos
20   de gargantas tiernas,
hechos bolatines,
andan sobre cuerdas.
Con vozes encantan,
con palabras pescan,
25   por ensalmo hartan

metric combination of any poet like those of a bank and, more so, if it does not suspend payment. Do not trust the hinge. Examine the door that, well oiled, waits for you without squeaking. Unburden yourself, if by chance you do not want that, while the page sings loudly and softly, the master takes advantage of the situation. Put another knot in your purse while they go around stealing. In Valladolid, there is no pretty gypsy girl who does not change her appearance by being still. Her foot on cork (look at what firmness) gracefully moves my honor and yours. To the sound of a tambourine, that she plays as she pleases, she consumes *cruzados;* that is a good coin. And, for the richest Count who dances with her, the Count of the gypsies leaves him without money. Put another knot in your purse while they go around stealing. They look at the palm of the hand that holds gifts of gold; the palm that does not is no good. They ruin lives, for even their wrists take undue liberties. From you, they acquire things from which to benefit, because women of this type make you see stars at midday. They look for your body, but, as they walk about, they will find your pockets first. Put another knot in your purse while they go around stealing. On four spans of a straight measure (rope), the merchant plays one hundred thousand tricks. With the feather in his ear, he flies through the world, giving strange jumps from one bazaar to another without fearing a fall, because, on silk, falls of a cat never caused pain. Bundles from Logroño can be loaded quickly, because, in order to commit frauds, one cleans out the store. Put another knot in your purse while they go around stealing. There are other gypsies of a better conscience, with healthy claws, without being great beasts, experts famous for making drills that bore into souls by acquiring wealth through deceit, for which purpose, they humbly manage out of holy passion the holy set of instruments, nails and claws, and for ascendance, then and now, the holy staircase. Put another knot in your purse while they go around stealing.

voluntades necias.
Y pues entonadas,
que aprendieron nueuas
entonadas damas
30   suelen dexar prendas.
Otro nudo a la bolsa
mientras que trepan.

Sobre sus dos manos
en su vara mesma,
35   mercader he visto,
que el cuerpo sustenta.
Yo he visto que en raso,
no aura quien lo crea,
anublar han hecho
40   muchas bolsas nueuas.
Pues a buelta de ojos
hazen tantas bueltas,
y solo no hazen
buelta en lo que lleuan.
45   Otro nudo a la bolsa
mientras que trepan.

(MADRIGAL: ENTRAMBASAGUAS, *Romancero general*, II, 50-51)

«Trepan los Gitanos» is dated 1603 in the Chacón manuscript, but Foulché-Delbosc assigns the date 1605 to the poem in his edition of the *Obras poéticas* (I, 260), claiming that Góngora, while in Valladolid in 1605, composed this and other verse about the Court.[6] The Millés and Jammes, however, support 1603 as the date of the text's composition in accordance with the Chacón manuscript.[7] Similarly, Artigas (p. 87) is skeptical about Foulché-Delbosc's theory; he notes there is no evidence that Góngora went to Valladolid in 1605 (p. 88), and he comments that the two poems that might justify such a trip, «Parió la Reina; el Lutherano vino» and «Abra dorada llaue», are not sufficient proof that such a journey took place.[8] However, it was not necessary for Góngora to have been in

---

[6] See the MILLÉS, pp. 1045-47, who state that Foulché-Delbosc believed that Góngora was in Valladolid in 1605, at which time the poet wrote «Trepan los Gitanos» and eleven other poems.

[7] The MILLÉS, p. 106, date the poem 1603 in their collection of Góngora's complete works, but they acknowledge Foulché-Delbosc's theory by placing this French critic's initials and the date 1605 in brackets after the 1603. JAMMES, *Études*, p. 105, writes: «La date donnée par Chacón (1603) ne me paraît pas devoir être mise en doute, puisque c'est celle du voyage de Góngora à Valladolid, et que ce *romancillo* s'intègre parfaitement dans l'ensemble des satires contre la Cour écrites en cette circonstance.»

[8] ARTIGAS, pp. 87-88, notes that Foulché-Delbosc attribues to Góngora the sonnet «Parió la Reina; el Lutherano vino», which commemorates the birth of Philip IV in 1605. Góngora's heroic song «Abra dorada llaue», on the same topic, is dated 1603 in the Chacón manuscript, but Foulché-Delbosc would more appropriately date

Valladolid to have written «Trepan los Gitanos». Moreover, I propose that this poem was composed in 1605, rather than in 1603, and that «Madrigal» is either a source of «Chacón», an earlier Góngora version of «Chacón», or a gloss of the same *villancico* composed at the same time as Góngora's *romancillo* by another poet participating in a contest with Góngora.[9] My reasoning is as follows:

1. Neither «Chacón», «Hoces», nor «Madrigal» appear in the *Romancero general* of 1600 published by Luis Sánchez or in the 1604 edition published by Juan de la Cuesta. But «Madrigal» is printed in González Palencia's edition of the *Romancero general,* which includes, from the original Madrigal edition, a copy of the frontispiece on which is visible the publication date 1605.[10] Foulché-Delbosc, in his «Bibliographie de Góngora» (p. 85), also states that Madrigal's collection was published in 1605. It is not likely then that, if Góngora had written «Chacón» or «Madrigal» in 1603, these versions would have been overlooked for publication in the 1604 edition of the *Romancero general* and would not have appeared in print before 1605, considering the popularity of Góngora's works and their wide circulation in oral and written form.[11]

2. The Madrigal version of the poem is clearly so inferior to the Chacón text that it must be either an earlier version of «Chacón» by Góngora, a source of «Chacón» by another poet, a gloss of the same *villancico* written at the same time as Góngora's *romancillo* by a mediocre poet, or a later imitation of «Chacón» by an admirer less talented than Góngora.

3. Madrigal claims that the version of «Trepan los Gitanos» included in his 1605 anthology had never been published before; he states the following in reference to his entire collection:

it 1605. Artigas, however, comments that the authorship of the sonnet is uncertain and that Góngora could have written the poem «Abra dorada llaue» in anticipation of the birth that was rumored as early as 1603 or merely to express Spain's longing for a prince. Although convinced that Góngora was in Valladolid in 1603 and doubtful that he was there in 1605, Artigas points out that the dates of the poems are indeed questionable. JAMMES, *Études*, pp. 57-58, n. 15, and the MILLÉS, p. 1064, like Artigas, question Góngora's authorship of the sonnet, but Juan Antonio Pellicer, who saw it attributed to Góngora in manuscript 14 of the Biblioteca Nacional (see ARTIGAS, p. 89) and who published it in volume one of his new corrected edition of MIGUEL DE CERVANTES SAAVEDRA's *El ingenioso hidalgo Don Quijote de la Mancha* (Madrid: Gabriel de Sancha, 1797), p. 115, believed Góngora wrote it, as did Tomé Pinheiro da Veiga who published it with a commentary in «Relación del bautismo de Felipe IV», in the *Fastiginia o fastos geniales,* trans. Narciso Alonso Cortés (Valladolid: Imprenta del Colegio de Santiago, 1916), pp. 2-3. Cf. CIPLIJAUSKAITÉ, *Sonetos,* p. 586.

   [9] ARTIGAS, pp. 142-43 and pp. 145-46, states that Góngora took part in poetry contests, either as a judge or as a participant.

   [10] See GONZÁLEZ PALENCIA, II, 205.

   [11] I know of no collection printed before 1605 in which either the Chacón or Madrigal version of «Trepan los Gitanos» appears. Even the *Primera parte de las flores de poetas ilustres de España,* which was completed in November of 1603 and published in 1605, does not contain either version among the many Góngora poems it reproduces. See the approbation on p. 4 of this anthology and JAMMES, *Études,* p. 275.

En la cual se contiene mucha variedad de romances, y otras rimas, que nunca hasta ahora han sido impresas.[12]

If, then, «Chacón» was written in 1603 or earlier, it would not only be unlikely that the Chacón version was not discovered and published before 1605, but also less likely that this text, so superior to «Madrigal», would have been published first, unless the reader accepts the theory that some unknown poet composed a poor imitation of «Chacón».

4. The possibility that «Madrigal» was written after «Chacón» by an imitator and the possibility that «Madrigal» is a gloss composed at the same time as «Chacón» by an inferior poet participating in a contest are probably not valid because:

  A. *Romanceros* and *cancioneros* often included verse by well-known poets without identifying them. Madrigal's collection reproduces anonymously other poems by Góngora, suggesting that «Madrigal» may indeed be a Góngora text.[13]
  B. Foulché-Delbosc, in his «Bibliographie de Góngora» (p. 85), lists «Trepan los Gitanos» as one of the Góngora poems that appear in Madrigal's 1605 anthology, and Jammes names Góngora as the author of «Trepan los Gitanos» and five other pieces printed in the same work.[14]

To further explain why I believe «Madrigal» to be an earlier version of «Chacón», I now turn to the texts themselves. «Chacón», «Hoces», and «Madrigal» begin with the *villancico,* the final two lines of which are repeated after each strophe:

> Trepan los Gitanos
> I bailan ellas,
> Otro nudo a la bolsa
> Mientras que trepan.
>
> (CHACÓN: FOULCHÉ-DELBOSC, I, 260, 1-4)

Here the reader encounters the poem's vivid sense of movement introduced by the verb «trepar», which is defined in the *Diccionario de Autoridades* as follows:

> Subir à algun lugar alto, áspero, ù dificultoso, valiendose y ayudandose de los pies, y las manos.[15]

---

[12] See GONZÁLEZ PALENCIA, II, 215.

[13] Five other poems by Góngora that appear in Madrigal's anthology are: «Despuntado he mil agujas», «Frescos airecillos», «La corza temerosa» (a variant of «Corcilla temerosa»), «Murmuraban los rocines», and «Ya de mi dulce instrumento». Cf. JAMMES, *Études,* p. 275.

[14] See note 13 above. JAMMES, *Études,* p. 105, however, states that he believes «Madrigal» to be a revision of «Chacón», although he gives no support for his belief. In addition, he comments he does not understand why the version of «Trepan los Gitanos» included in Madrigal's anthology has only three strophes that are, except for similar content, very different from the seven of the Chacón text.

[15] S.v. «trepar», III, pt. 6, 350.

The verb has also been interpreted as meaning «pasar la maroma», «hacer acrobacia», «voltear por el aire como volatinero», «pisar», «patalear», «retozar», «patear», «saltar», and «danzar».[16] «Trepar's» association with other expressions in the poem makes such meanings appropriate throughout the text. «Dar bueltas en la rueda de Fortuna» refers to climbing, whereas «bailar», «dar bueltas», «andar (caminar) de manos», «hacer ligerezas», and «dar brincos» suggest turns, handstands, steps, leaps, kicks, skips, and other acrobatic or dance activities. Some verbs or phrases found in «Madrigal», such as «dar vueltas», «hurtar», «volar de ligeros», «hechos volatines», «andar sobre cuerdas», and «anublar bolsas», when used in conjunction with «trepar», evoke the lively dances of the gypsies and their dexterity in stealing. The poem, however, emphasizes that «Chacón's» gypsies of the Court (finagling courtiers) or «Madrigal's» gypsies of the world (pilfering tricksters) were assiduously trying to «climb» and maneuver their way to a better financial status by using all of their resources, including their feet and hands.

The twirling, tumbling, and springing movements of the work are set to a background of musical terms and images. These visually powerful images subdue the poetic structure that contains them by metaphorically transforming the text into a pattern of dance movements, a figure constituting a *mudanza,* which conjures up the verses' lively atmosphere.[17] This figure combines popular and stylized techniques within the poem's brisk tempo, but the rhythmic and musical impressions, so noteworthy in «Chacón», are not as significant in «Madrigal». The treatment of sound and movement, an integral part of both versions, is only really effective within the context of the longer work. The following antithesis illustrates how «Chacón» is particularly expressive of movement:

> En Valladolid
> 60 No ay Gitana bella
> Que no haga mudanças
> Estandose queda.
>
> (CHACÓN: FOULCHÉ-DELBOSC, I, 262)

From the contrast evoked by the phrase «estandose queda» and the word «mudanças»[18] the reader infers more than the significance of the dance

---

[16] COROMINAS, IV (Berna: Francke, 1954), p. 565, s.v. «trepar», I.

[17] In «A Dialectic of Aural and Objective Correlatives», in *Perspectives on Poetry*, ed. James L. Calderwood and Harold E. Toliver (New York: Oxford University Press, 1968), Father Walter Ong comments that Archibald MacLeish, in his «Ars Poetica», manifests visual and tactile biases in the comparison of a poem to a series of visually and tactually oriented objects (i.e., «A poem should be wordless / As the flight of birds») (p. 120). Góngora manifests a similar bias toward visual images in his poetry, creating the illusion they are part of his poem that, in turn, represents either some other form of art (i.e., a painting, a statue, or a dance).

[18] *Diccionario de Autoridades*, II, pt. 4, 623: «MUDANZA. Se llama tambien cierto

figure. The meaning of these verses is that the dexterity of the gypsies (courtiers) promotes their stealing even while they remain in one spot, ironically alluding to the ineptitude of the Spanish people to cope with gypsies and similar confidence tricksters. Góngora's antithesis, however, also suggests a completely different interpretation; it pays tribute to the beauty of art (the dance) and nature (the gypsy woman) that causes changes in the beholder even when that beauty is in repose (not dancing).[19]

The Chacón poem, then, is about those who dwell in the Court and exploit their place of residence for a living by cheating and beguiling like gypsies. The theme and the poem's emphasis on sound are most adeptly integrated in strophes two to four of the Chacón text (23-76). In strophe two (23-40), for example, a courtier's sweet song, analogous to that of a nightingale, flatters an unwitting victim as a gypsylike accomplice picks the unsuspecting one's pocket.

The allusions to music in the shorter version, however, are neither as complex nor as extensive as those belonging to «Chacón». Strophe two of «Madrigal» includes the observation, made in «Chacón», that the gypsylike members of society are able to charm their prey with song. In addition, this strophe draws a parallel between the dexterity of such thieves in walking the tightrope and their agility in manipulating watch chains or in playing a stringed instrument:

> Cantores con passos
> 20 de gargantas tiernas,
> hechos bolatines,
> andan sobre cuerdas.

Again, in the same strophe, the gypsies of the world blandish their victims out of whom they wheedle money or gifts:

> Con vozes encantan,
> con palabras pescan,
> 25 por ensalmo hartan
> voluntades necias.

The focal point of «Madrigal's» last four lines emphasizes sound and movement. In these verses, t's and some d stops are intermingled with s's.

número de movimientos, que se hace en los bailes y danzas, arreglado al tañido de los instrumentos. Lat. *Saltatoria mutatio, varietas.* Cerv. Quix. tom. 2. cap. 20. Comenzaba la danza del Cupido, y habiendo hecho dos *mudanzas,* alzaba los ojos y hechaba el arco contra una doncella, que se ponia entre las almenas del Castillo. Cald. Com. El Maestro de danzar. Jorn. 2: '... que sabrá presto / quanto hai que saber, porque / à la primer licion veo, / que ha hecho toda una mudanza.'»

[19] JORGE GUILLÉN, *Language and Poetry* (Cambridge, MA: Harvard University Press, 1961), p. 51: «Góngora takes shelter in robust quietness. Or, if it moves, its unstable aspect is allied to a metaphor of stability: ... A world in repose, or in a repose indicating change, like the gypsy girls of Valladolid.» Guillén cites the four verses beginning «En Valladolid...» to support his point.

The resulting effect is a fluid dance rhythm created by the s's and a brisk tempo produced by the harsh sounds of the t's and d stops:

> Y pues entonadas,
> que aprendieron nueuas
> entonadas damas
> 30   suelen dexar prendas.

The wordplay on «en tonadas» (in songs) and «entonadas» (arrogant) instills an additional element of wit into the musical games, but «Madrigal» cannot compete with Góngora's melding of vibrant movement and clear tones with his subject matter, a skill so expertly demonstrated in «Chacón's» fourth strophe:

> En Valladolid
> 60   No ay Gitana bella
> Que no haga mudanças
> Estandose queda.
> El pie sobre corcho
> (Mirad que firmeza)
> 65   Mueue con buen aire
> Mi honra, i la vuestra.
> Al son de vn pandero,
> Que a su gusto suena,
> Deshaze cruzados,
> 70   Que es buena moneda.
> I al Conde mas rico,
> Que bayla con ella,
> Conde de Gitanos,
> Desnudo le dexa.
> 75   Otro nudo a la bolsa
>   Mientras que trepan.
>
> (CHACÓN: FOULCHÉ-DELBOSC, I, 262)

In these simultaneously lively and graceful dancelike verses, Góngora blends the motif of rhythmic movement and the sounds of fricatives and stops with the theme of gypsy agility. The effect is that «Chacón», unlike «Madrigal», has overcome the paradoxical relationship between content and form that is exaggerated by many writers of Baroque literature;[20] the content and form of «Chacón» are remarkably alike. Furthermore, the constant interaction between the visual (form) and the abstract (content) is the principal appeal of these, like many of Góngora's other verses.[21]

[20] RENÉ WELLEK, «The Concept of the Baroque in Literary Scholarship», in *Concepts of Criticism*, ed. Stephen G. Nichols, Jr. (New Haven: Yale University Press, 1963), p. 110, discusses this relationship.

[21] KARL VOSSLER, *Formas poéticas de los pueblos románicos* (Buenos Aires: Losada, 1960), p. 91, explains it is a «flujo y reflujo constante entre cuadros visuales e ideas abstractas, con lo que resulta una especie de juegos de acertijos» that is the major poetic technique of Gongorists and Marinists.

Even the conclusions of the poems demonstrate the inferiority of the Madrigal text, which ends on a carefree note:

> Pues a buelta de ojos
> hazen tantas bueltas,
> y solo no hazen
> buelta en lo que lleuan.
>
> (41-44)

Through their wordplay, these verses state that the merchants haggle about prices:

> VUELTA. Se toma tambien por la demasia que se le debe volver al que compra, ò trueca alguna cosa respecto del precio concertado.[22]

The secondary meaning of «vuelta» is the 360 degree leap of an acrobatic dancer, such as a gypsy. The implication is that the only gypsy activity that does not include a «turn» involves their stolen property; it is not «returned».

The whimsical tone of the Madrigal poem quickly yields to a moralizing note in the final strophe of «Chacón»:

> Ay otros Gitanos
> De mejor conciencia,
> 115 Saludables de vñas,
> Sin ser grandes bestias,
> Maestros famosos
> De hazer barrenas,
> Que taladran almas,
> 120 Por clauar haziendas;
> Para cuio fin
> Humildes menéàn
> De la passion santa
> La santa herramienta,
> 125 Clauos, i tenaças,
> I para ascendencia
> De años a esta parte
> La santa escalera.
> Otro nudo a la bolsa
> 130 Mientras que trepan.
>
> (CHACÓN: FOULCHÉ-DELBOSC, I, 263-64)

«Chacón» makes the point that, besides the sophisticates of the Court, ecclesiastics have also adopted gypsylike behavior. What is worse, these hypocrites pilfer souls and employ religion for profit. The holy ladder for ascension into heaven becomes, for them, a rope to facilitate their thievish endeavors.

---

[22] *Diccionario de Autoridades*, III, pt. 6, 527.

Some critics have claimed that Góngora composed the last strophe of «Chacón» as an unexpected attack on the Jesuits.[23] Jammes points out that the attack is surprising after the previous butts of ridicule: «prétendants, séducteurs, courtisans, marchands» (p. 105). The Alonso-Galvarriato documents, which include excerpts from the testament and inventory of Juan de Argote y Sepúlveda, Góngora's brother-in-law, «donnent sa pleine résonance à la dernière strophe du *romance* 'Trepan los gitanos'».[24] When Juan de Argote died on 24 April 1617, his Jesuit confessor, Padre Diego de Córdoba, who was named as an inheritor, managed to usurp a portion of the Argote fortune.[25] Góngora's criticism of the Jesuits, then, suggests censorship as the reason why the poem's final strophe does not appear in «Hoces», which is otherwise the same as «Chacón». This hypothesis is strengthened by Vicuña's inclusion of the final strophe in his version of Góngora's text. Vicuña strongly resisted the inquisitorial censorship to which his collection was subjected:

> Chose incroyable, Pineda et Horio n'ont rien dit (ou rien voulu dire?) de cette strophe, qui figure pourtant bel et bien dans l'édition Vicuña; il n'en reste pas moins qu'elle fut supprimée dans l'édition Hoces, peut-être sur l'initiative de l'éditeur lui-même, qui semble avoir joué une partie très serrée contre les censeurs de l'Inquisition.[26]

«Chacón's» final strophe does not appear in «Madrigal» because it, too, may have been censored or because «Madrigal» was most probably a source or earlier version of «Chacón», and «Chacón's» final strophe would not have been written until after the completion of «Madrigal». However, «Madrigal» could have been a gloss of the *villancico* «Trepan los Gitanos» written by an unknown poet at the same time as Góngora's *romancillo*.

The main point of «Chacón», which is to criticize the vices of the Court and, as a parting shot, the transgressions of ecclesiastics, is completely lost in «Madrigal». The Madrigal verse «Gitanos del mundo» weakens the intensity of the poet's attack on the courtiers by extending it to include not only the gypsies of the Court, but also those of the world. Without «Chacón's» final strophe, the poem degenerates into a mere series of fraudulent activities. The themes of deception and money and the motifs of sound and movement unify the text, preparing the reader for its coda, Góngora's satirical point. If the coda is suppressed, the poetic devices that enhance the work's attributes and emphasize its main theme lose their direction, failing to reach a climax and ending the poem abruptly and inconclusively.

---

[23] See JAMMES, *Études*, p. 105.
[24] DÁMASO ALONSO and EULALIA GALVARRIATO DE ALONSO, eds., *Para la biografía de Góngora: documentos desconocidos* (Madrid: Gredos, 1962), pp. 353 and 382, *apud* JAMMES, *Études*, p. 107, n. 124.
[25] JAMMES, *Études*, p. 107, n. 124.
[26] JAMMES, *Études*, p. 107, n. 124.

The Madrigal version is then so inferior to the Chacón text that it is not likely to be a later version of «Chacón» by Góngora or an imitation of Góngora's *romancillo* by an unknown poet who thought he could improve on the verse of a master. An analysis of both texts of «Trepan los Gitanos» and the available information about them suggest that, at the very least, the Madrigal version is an anonymous source of Góngora's poem or a gloss of the *villancico* «Trepan los Gitanos» written by an inferior poet at the same time that Góngora composed his *romancillo*. «Madrigal», however, may well be an earlier Góngora version of «Chacón».

Imitations of a poet's works are often created by his admirers, but some purported imitations may turn out to be sources for his verse. Others may even be a poet's actual earlier versions of his later texts. Yet still others are surely glosses by poets participating in contest. In the Spanish Golden Age, the question of imitation regarding poems such as «Trepan los Gitanos» was, whenever possible, answered by the issues of authorship and chronology.

V

CONCLUDING REMARKS

The vast corpus of Góngora's poetry with its numerous variants, versions, and imitations raises the fundamental issues of authenticity and authorship. The works included in the Chacón manuscript, the definitive collection of Góngora's shorter poems, are authentic, although Chacón notes that some texts are partly composed of apocryphal verses. Which of the variants, versions, and imitations of these poems are genuine Góngora compositions? Which have authentic or apocryphal strophes and lines?

Few critics have dealt with these important questions. Some have noted variant texts or verses, but most have written about the possible Góngora authorship of poems that do not appear in the Chacón manuscript. For example, Ciplijauskaité's edition of Góngora's *Sonetos,* which includes an extensive catalogue of textual variants, also contains a section of sonnets incorrectly attributed to Góngora (pp. 614-71) and a list of some poems previously credited to him with the name of the real author of each text printed below its first line (pp. 672-75). Many sonnets that critics have thought to be by Góngora figure in her anthology (pp. 572-613). Similarly, Dámaso Alonso has written on the topic of false attribution; in his *Estudios y ensayos gongorinos,* he explains why the poem «El Duque mi señor se fué a Francía» is not Góngora's work (pp. 263-75). Moreover, Foulché-Delbosc records the first lines of poems attributed to Góngora in volume three of his edition of the *Obras poéticas* (pp. 127-36). In the heading of his list, he mentions that some of these poems may be authentic whereas others are erroneously assigned to Góngora (p. 127).

Chacón, however, confronts the problem of verifiability in his manuscript collection of Góngora's poetry by acknowledging that he cannot confirm the authenticity of all of the verses of all of the texts included in this anthology. Furthermore, Chacón occasionally notes that some works are incomplete:

> Así, en el manuscrito Chacón hay varias composiciones incompletas: ya falta una estrofa o dos, ya aparece una nota que señala la falta de algunos versos: «No se ha podido hallar quien los tenga.»[1]

---

[1] FOULCHÉ-DELBOSC, I, xii.

Clearly, if the authorship of Góngora's poems or parts of them is questionable, the reader will find that distinguishing among the many authentic and apocryphal variants and versions of these texts is a difficult task:

> Los editores de Góngora se encuentran, así, a la vista de multitud de manuscritos gongorinos llenos de variantes, muchas de ellas de fuente legítima, como se encuentran los recopiladores de canciones y temas de la feria y la plaza ante versiones diferentes que andan de boca en boca.[2]

Whereas some variants and versions of Góngora's works are likely to be revisions by later poets, adulterated transcriptions, or apocryphal texts, others may be or may reflect genuine Góngora compositions. Imitations, in addition, may be either Góngora's admirers' creations or the poet's own art inspired by that of his predecessors.

Why, however, is it important to study the variants, versions, and imitations of Góngora's work? What do they tell us about his poetry? First of all, although vast and complex, they are not so elusive that an in-depth analysis of them cannot resolve some of the problems of Góngora's poetic textual tradition. Their study not only contributes greatly to perfecting his official canon, but it also serves as a model for amending and completing the verse of other major poets of the Spanish Golden Age. Second, given Góngora's propensity for revision, some authentic versions help to establish or correct dates of poems in the Chacón collection. Third, a study of variants, versions, and imitations allows the reader to gain insight into Góngora's creative process. Such is the case with the Portuguese version of «Grandes mas que elephantes i que habadas», which most likely reflects an earlier Góngora text. The versions of other poems that may well be original drafts of later Góngora compositions may also shed light on the poet's craftsmanship. Forth, some of Góngora's poems have apocryphal conclusions, are truncated, or are missing strophes. To find among the plethora of extant texts the authentic endings and lost strophes of Góngora's poems is to complete both his individual works and the Chacón anthology. Finally, the determination of the authorship of a version or imitation of a piece adds the finishing touches to Góngora's poetic canon and enriches the larger body of Spanish Golden Age poetry.

---

[2] ALFONSO REYES, *Trazos de historia literaria,* 2nd ed. (Buenos Aires: Espasa-Calpe, 1951), pp. 115-16.

APPENDIX

SOME VERSIONS AND IMITATIONS: INCONCLUSIVE EVIDENCE

Although some variants and versions of Góngora's work are nothing more than revisions or imitations by later poets, adulterated transcriptions, or spurious texts, others are obvious reflections or copies of authentic poems. The reader of Góngora's verse, while gaining much insight into the poet's works, sometimes remains confused regarding which of the variants and versions are really by Góngora.

A) «LOS RAIOS LE QUENTA AL SOL»: TWO VERSIONS

When studying some of Góngora's poems such as the amorous *romance* «Los raios le quenta al Sol», the reader is inclined to ask whether a poem is an imitation or an original text. The theme of this poem is very similar to that of a Spanish sonnet collected by Antonio Alvares da Cunha and attributed to Luiz de Camões in the 1668 edition of the *Rimas*. The poem, «Á la margen del Tajo, en claro dia», is about a young lady, Natercia, who, while combing her hair on the banks of the Tajo, causes the sun to lose its brilliance by the gleam in her eyes.[1] Góngora's sonnet, «Al Sol peinaua Clori sus cabellos», treats the same topic,[2] and his longer piece, «Los raios le quenta al Sol», deals with a variation of this theme. The *romance* has two known versions; one appears in the Chacón manuscript,[3] and the other, listed under Góngora's name in a manuscript owned by José María de Alava, a professor at the University of Seville, is reproduced in volume forty-two of the BAE[4] (1875):

---

[1] FUCILLA, «A Decade», p. 41. On the next page, Fucilla cites the poem from volume III of CAMÕES's *Rimas* (Lisboa: Na Officina de Antonio Craesbeeck de Mello, 1668) apud the *Obras completas* (Porto: Imprensa Portugueza, 1873), I, 123.

[2] See FUCILLA, «A Decade», pp. 41-42.

[3] See FOULCHÉ-DELBOSC, I, 5.

[4] Ed. Rivadeneyra, 2nd ed. (Madrid: Sucesores de Rivadeneyra), p. 596. Rivadeneyra states on the same page that the manuscript from which the poem was reproduced was owned by José María de Alava, but he gives no more information about this professor, the manuscript, or the poem.

Los raios le quenta al Sol
Con vn peine de marfil
La bella IACINTA, vn dia
Que por mi dicha la vi
5   En la verde orilla
De Guadalquiuir.

La mano obscurece al peine;
Mas, que mucho? si el Abril
La viò obscurecer los lilios
10   Que blancos suelen salir
En la verde orilla
De Guadalquiuir.

Los paxaros la saludan,
Porque piensan, (i es assi),
15   Que el Sol que sale en Oriente
Buelue otra vez a salir
En la verde orilla
De Guadalquiuir.

Por solo un cabello el Sol
20   De sus raios diera mil,
Solicitando inuidioso
El que se quedaua alli,
En la verde orilla
De Guadalquiuir.

(CHACÓN: FOULCHÉ-DELBOSC, I, 5)[5]

Los rayos le cuenta al sol
Con un peine de marfil
La bella Jacinta, un dia
Que por mi dicha la vi
5   En la verde orilla del Guadalquivir.

Y porque tantos no tenga
Con que matar y herir,
Quita al peine algunos de ellos,
Y siémbralos por allí
10   En la verde orilla del Guadalquivir.

Resuena en las arboledas
El airecillo sutil;
Ya murmura entre las ramas,

---

[5] My translation of the Chacón version of «Los raios le quenta al Sol» appears here: One day, by my good fortune, I saw the beautiful Jacinta combing her golden hair with ivory on the green banks of the Guadalquivir. Her hand eclipses her comb. But, is that surprising since April saw her hand eclipse the white lilies that usually bloom on the green banks of the Guadalquivir? The birds greet her because they think (and so it is) that the sun that rises in the Orient rises again on the green banks of the Guadalquivir. For only one hair, the sun would give a thousand of its rays, soliciting enviously the one strand that remained there on the green banks of the Guadalquivir.

Ya vuelve á entrar, ya á salir,
15 En la verde orilla del Guadalquivir.

Cantan las aves, alegres
De ver otro sol salir,
Muy mas claro y mas hermoso
Que el que las solia cubrir
20 En la verde orilla del Guadalquivir.

Venid ya, ninfas hermosas,
Las que mi pena sentis,
Y en las sienes de Jacinta
Una guirnalda ceñid
25 En la verde orilla del Guadalquivir.

De las mas floridas flores
Que el alba suele vestir
Entretejed entre rosas
Lo verde de toronjil
30 En la verde orilla del Guadalquivir.

Y cuando vais á ponerla,
Por mí lo podréis decir,
Que esperanzas me entretienen,
Porque jamás tendrán fin
35 En la verde orilla del Guadalquivir.

(BAE, XLII, 596)

Dated 1580 in the Chacón manuscript, the short text of the *romance* is composed of four strophes, each of which is followed by the refrain «En la verde orilla / De Guadalquiuir». A note in the Chacón manuscript, however, explains that «Solo este primer quartete i la buelta, es suyo [de Góngora]; pero siguiole tan bien quien lo continuò, que se pone aqui con esta aduertencia».[6] Francisco García Lorca did not take this note seriously; in his article, «Análisis de un *romance* de Góngora», published in the *Romanic Review*,[7] he discusses the poem as it appears in the Chacón manuscript, concluding that the *romance* is not in part an imitation of Góngora's style by an unknown poet but rather a genuine Góngora composition: «A pesar de la autoridad, no ciertamente infalible, del manuscrito Chacón, creo haber reforzado la presunción de que todo el poema es de mano de Góngora» (p. 26).

The analysis on which García Lorca bases his conclusion that the entire poem is Góngora's work is largely a study of the text's assonance, alliteration, rhythm, and thematic correlation. The critic acknowledges the poem exists in more than one version, but he states he is only interested in attending to the one found in the Chacón manuscript (p. 14). Although illuminating, García Lorca's study unconvincingly concludes that Góngora

---

[6] FOULCHÉ-DELBOSC, I, 5.
[7] 47 (1956), 13-26.

is the author of the entire Chacón text. Many of the observations García Lorca makes in his analysis of the Chacón version, such as the correlation of the assonance in the Góngora strophe with the assonance in the other strophes of the *romance,* are similarly applicable to the long and quite distinctive version of the poem printed in the BAE. Thus, the reasons that lead García Lorca to argue the Chacón text is by Góngora would probably have led him to argue that Góngora wrote the BAE text, if the critic had studied the long instead of the short version.

Clearly, Góngora was unable to find his *romance* when assisting in the compilation of the Chacón manuscript because Chacón collected a short imitation of the piece written by an unknown poet. Probably recognizing the first strophe of the short piece as his work and pleased by the way in which the unknown poet completed the text, Góngora allowed Chacón to include this version in the manuscript with the note that strophes two, three, and four were apocryphal. Because the Chacón manuscript, although not infallible, was compiled by Chacón with the assistance of Góngora, the reader has no reason to doubt Chacón's note that the short version is not entirely by Góngora.

However, one question remains: Is the long version Góngora's work? In analyzing the BAE text, the reader finds it is similar to that of the Chacón manuscript. A study of the BAE version's assonance, alliteration, rhythm, and theme, however, reveals little about authorship. Both the BAE and Chacón versions have essentially the same first strophe. García Lorca explains that the second strophe of the Chacón text has six verses with the final accent on «i» or «ei» («peine», «Abril», «lilios», «salir», «orilla», «Guadalquiuir»), with «l-ll» alliteration, and with «s» repetition.[8] The preponderance of the letters «r» and «e» is also obvious. The BAE poem consists of six verses with the final accent on «i» or «e» («tenga», «herir», «ellos», «allí», «orilla», «Guadalquivir»), and each line repeats one or more of the following consonants: «t», «s», «r», «l», and «ll». All of the strophes of both versions have «i» assonance, «s», «l», «ll», and «r» sounds, and repetition of the letter «t», which is, however, more prominent in the strophes of the BAE text. The vowels «a», «o», and «i» dominate the first strophe of both versions, and although these vowels appear in the other strophes of the two texts, the vowel «e» and «e-a» assonance is prevalent. Either «a», «o», or «a-o» sounds are noticeable in the first line of each strophe in the Chacón and BAE versions.

The theme of the Chacón text is the beauty of Jacinta, a young maiden. In describing her, the verses of the Chacón piece include three nouns, «raios» («cabellos»), «Sol» («Jacinta»), and «peine» («marfil») in the first strophe, and the remaining three strophes each contain one of these nouns,

---

[8] GARCÍA LORCA, pp. 15-16 and 18.

only in reverse order: strophe two, «peine», strophe three, «Sol», and strophe four, «raios».[9] Whiteness/light, a leitmotiv representing beauty in Góngora's *Las soledades,* is dominant in the Chacón text. Jacinta's hand, which hides her ivory comb, is implicit in the first two verses of the poem and introduces into the text the concept of whiteness that is expressed throughout the first two strophes by such words as «mano», «marfil», «lilios», and «blancos».[10] Metaphors involving light and radiance, and thus the colors yellow and gold — «raios» («cabellos») and «Sol» («Jacinta») —complement those of whiteness. Consequently, the concepts of purity and light are continued into the final strophe where the metaphor of «Jacinta» («Sol») is disassociated;[11] Jacinta is now a new «Sol» that rivals the old one. The continuity of the poem and its metaphors, however, is reinforced by the whiteness and light that enhance Jacinta's beauty and by the refrain that unifies the *romance*'s strophes. More than emphatic, the refrain includes mention of the Guadalquivir that metaphorically reflects the scene of each strophe it succeeds.[12]

The imagery of the BAE version of «Los raios le quenta al Sol» is different from that found in the Chacón text, but this version is also well unified thematically. Strophe one of the BAE text is identical to strophe one in the short version (except for its modernized spelling, capitalization, and use of the contraction «del») and thus includes the same three metaphors, «rayos» («cabellos»), «sol» («Jacinta»), «peine» («marfil»), and the same refrain, «En la verde orilla del Guadalquivir». Strophes two to seven in the BAE version describe Jacinta and the poem's setting at the banks of the river. Unlike the text in the Chacón manuscript, which concentrates mostly on Jacinta seated at the river's edge, the BAE version depicts the young lady and the scene around her. The background and action of the scene are combined in the BAE text with the result that each strophe is like a picture in continual motion. Together the strophes form a series of tableaux that appear, one at a time, before the reader's eyes and move slowly toward the poem's conclusion. Strophe one of the BAE text introduces Jacinta as she combs her hair on the banks of the river, and strophe two focuses on the beauty of her hair («rayos») and on her ivory comb («peine»). Strophe three describes the breeze that blows in and out of the groves near the maiden as it murmurs among the tree branches at the banks of the Guadalquivir, strophe four depicts the birds happy that a new sun (Jacinta), which is brighter and more beautiful than

[9] García Lorca, p. 25.

[10] Cf. Walter Pabst, *La creación gongorina en los poemas «Polifemo» y «Soledades»*, trans. Nicolás Marín (Madrid: CSIC, 1966), p. 91, who discusses light as a leitmotiv in *Las soledades*. See also García Lorca, p. 25, who comments on the role of whiteness in the Chacón text of «Los raios le quenta al Sol».

[11] García Lorca, p. 25.

[12] García Lorca, pp. 25-26.

the sun to which they are accustomed, is shining on them, strophe five introduces the nymphs who will make a floral crown for the lovely maiden's head, strophe six details the garland that will be made of roses and jonquils, and strophe seven comments on the coronation of Jacinta and on the poet's unfulfilled hopes concerning this lady of his dreams. The BAE version, then, includes the same three images as the Chacón text («peine», «rayos», and «sol»), not in reverse order, but in an order conforming to the poet's description of the maiden and her surroundings.

Color plays a significant role in «Los raios le quenta al Sol». White and gold/yellow found in the Chacón version contrast with red and green, which appear in the BAE text. According to Walter Pabst, the four colors visible in Góngora's poetry are, in order of importance, white, red, green, and gold, colors also characteristic of Renaissance poetry.[13] Yellow, although not as common, is a variant of gold often associated with light and therefore noticeable in the verse of Góngora who, like Herrera, often employed white and light to portray feminine beauty.[14] Whereas in the Chacón text white and gold/yellow are the dominant colors, in the BAE text, white and gold/yellow depict Jacinta, her hair, her hand, the temples of her head, her comb, and the jonquils in her crown; green is evoked by the trees, the riverbanks, and Jacinta's garland; red is alluded to by the roses of the crown, the wounds of love indicated by the verbs «matar» and «herir», and the poet's metaphorical bleeding heart and spiritual death (the consequences of his unrequited love), and finally a rainbow of tones is suggested by the birds and flowers of the countryside.

Besides color, sound is important to Góngora's poetry; it refers not only to the musicality of the verses, but to the images and vocabulary with which the poet conjures up, for example, singing birds, running water, or the wind rustling the leaves of the trees.[15] In the Chacón text of «Los raios le quenta al Sol», the only possible allusions to sound are the reference to the birds that greet Jacinta in strophe three and the mention of the sun that solicits one of her hairs in strophe four. In the BAE text, however, more sound is evoked by the employment of descriptive verbs. The breeze echoes («resuena») and murmurs («murmura») in the groves as it blows through the branches of the trees («Ya vuelve á entrar, ya á salir»). The

[13] PABST, pp. 92-93. See also JOSÉ ARES MONTES, Góngora y la poesía portuguesa del siglo XVII (Madrid: Gredos, 1956), p. 304, who notes that these four colors, most commonly found in Renaissance poetry, are also found in the verse of Camões.
[14] Cf. PABST, p. 96, who explains that yellow, which like beige is a shade of gold, is sometimes represented by ivory. In «Los raios le quenta al Sol», however, «marfil» suggests whiteness. PABST, p. 92, cites Herrera's sonnet «Ahora, que cubrió de blanco hielo» from JOSÉ MARÍA COSSÍO's article «Candores, esplendores», RO, 4, No. 40 (1926), 112. According to Pabst, Herrera's poem is a «sinfonía de blanco y luz».
[15] ARES MONTES, p. 308, explains the role of sound in Góngora's poetry.

birds sing happily («Cantan las aves, alegres») as they rejoice at the sight of Jacinta, and the poet expresses his feelings of love towards her when he asks the nymphs to speak to her on his behalf («Por mí lo podréis decir»).

Metaphor and allusion, often employed by Góngora, are combined in the two versions of «Los raios le quenta al Sol». In Chacón's version, «raios» = «cabellos», «Sol» = «Jacinta», and «marfil» = «peine». In addition to these three examples common to both poems, the Chacón text includes two others: «Abril» = this month personified, and the birds = the heralds of spring. In the BAE text, «rayos» = «cabellos», «sol» = «Jacinta», «marfil» = «peine», «arboledas» and «ramas» = nature's instruments by which the «airecillo» produces its music, «Jacinta» = a symbol of divine and natural beauty, the nymphs = woodland goddesses who are Jacinta's attendants, the «alba» = the dawn personified as a lady dressed in a floral gown, and the roses and jonquils = a wreath for Jacinta's head. In both versions, Jacinta is strongly linked to her environment through metaphor and allusion.

Bifurcation, a technique characteristic of much of Góngora's poetry, appears in the Chacón and BAE texts where it is manifested through parallelism, contrast, or gradation.[16] Bifurcation is expressed in the Chacón version in two examples of parallelism (7-9 and 15-16) and in the BAE text in two examples of contrast (6-8 and 17-19) and one of parallelism (11-13). The examples of bifurcation from both versions are used for intensification and amplification. The Chacón text's second strophe enhances the whiteness of Jacinta's skin; her hand eclipses first her ivory comb and then April's lilies. The third Chacón stanza likens the lady to the sun and, by extension, to joy, light, and the dawn. Through parallelism, the poet of the BAE version highlights the subtleness of the woodland breeze by comparing it to a gentle stream of air, and through contrast, he stresses the power of Jacinta's beauty by emphasizing the force of her many golden hairs over that of the beams of sunlight. Her hairs, rays of a brighter and more elegant sun (herself), have the energy to kill or wound with love.

Clearly, an analysis of the Chacón version of «Los raios le quenta al Sol» does not provide enough information to attribute its authorship to Góngora. Again the reader must accept the poet's statement that only the first strophe and the refrain of the *romance* are his and that some able poet finished the piece. The BAE text, which may have been composed by the same poet who wrote the Chacón version, by another poet, or by Góngora, demonstrates the style and many of the techniques found in the Chacón work and in much of Góngora's verse. Nevertheless, in this case, a study

---

16 PABST, pp. 33-37, discusses bifurcation, which is the expression of an idea in two separate parallel, gradational, and/or antithetical parts. Bifurcation sometimes includes wordplay and conceits.

of both texts' style and theme is not sufficiently conclusive to confirm Góngora as the author of either version.

B) THREE «HERMANOS»: MARICA, PERICO, AND JUANILLA

The Góngora *romancillo burlesco,* «Hermana Marica», was a prototype for other similar poems. At first glance, the *romancillo* seems to be narrated by a child who, in direct and juvenile language, describes to his sister his anticipation of a forthcoming holiday. Rather than attend school that day, the siblings will participate in morning church services and then enjoy the entertainment of the afternoon's events. Góngora speaks from within a child to reflect an autobiographical moment in his youth.[17] Except in the case of the *pícaros,* who are older people writing fictionally about their childhood, this technique is innovative in the literature of the Golden Age.[18] Although the historical person is absent from Góngora's poem, it is true that, on occasion, Góngora included himself in his youthful poetry.[19]

«Hermana Marica» was originally thought to have been written to imitate an anonymous poem beginning «Hermano Perico».[20] This theory of Menéndez y Pelayo, however, is no longer held to be true, and at present «Hermano Perico» is considered to be an imitation and parody of Góngora's «Hermana Marica».[21] The two poems are as follows:

> Hermana Marica,
> Mañana, que es fiesta,
> No iràs tu a la amiga,
> Ni io irè a la escuela.
> 5 Pondraste el corpiño
> I la saia buena,
> Cabezon labrado,
> Toca, i albanega;
> I a mi me pondran
> 10 Mi camisa nueua,
> Saio de palmilla,
> Media de estameña;
> I si hace bueno
> Trairè la montera

---

[17] MIGUEL ARTIGAS, *Semblanza de Góngora* (Madrid: Blass, 1928), p. 8, makes the following statement pertinent to the autobiographical character of Góngora's poem: the boys with whom Góngora played in his youth «serían de los treinta del barrio que jugaban con él al toro en la plazuela en los días de fiesta y a los que recuerda en el romance: 'Hermana Marica / mañana que es fiesta'».

[18] EMILIO CARILLA, «Notas gongorinas», *RFE,* 45 (1962), 32.

[19] See CARILLA, p. 33. Cf. GUILLÉN, p. 55.

[20] MARCELINO MENÉNDEZ Y PELAYO, *Estudios de crítica histórica y literaria* (Buenos Aires: Espasa-Calpe, 1944), I, 282-83.

[21] CARILLA, p. 35.

15   Que me diò la Pascua
        Mi señora abuela,
     I el estadal roxo
        Con lo que le cuelga,
        Que traxo el vecino
20   Quando fue a la feria.
     Iremos a Missa,
        Veremos la Iglesia,
        Darànos vn quarto
        Mi tia la ollera.
25   Comprarèmos de el,
        (Que nadie lo sepa),
        Chochos i garbanços
        Para la merienda;
     I en la tardecica,
30   En nuestra plaçuela,
        Iugarè io al toro
        I tu a las muñecas
     Con las dos hermanas,
        Iuana i Madalena,
35   I las dos primillas,
        Marica i la tuerta;
     I si quiere madre
        Dar las castañetas,
        Podràs tanto dello
40   Bailar en la puerta;
     I al son del adufe
        Cantarà Andrehuela:
        «No me aprouecharon,
        Madre, las hierbas»;
45   I io de papel
        Harè vna librea,
        Teñida con moras
        Porque bien parezca,
     I vna caperuza
50   Con muchas almenas;
        Pondrè por penacho
        Las dos plumas negras
     Del rabo del gallo,
        Que acullà en la huerta
55   Anaranjéàmos
        Las Carnestolendas;
     I en la caña larga
        Pondrè vna vandera
        Con dos borlas blancas
60   En sus trançaderas;
     I en mi cauallito
        Pondrè vna cabeza
        De guadameci,
        Dos hilos por riendas;
65   I entrarè en la calle
        Haciendo corbetas

Io i otros del barrio,
Que son mas de treinta.
Iugaremos cañas
70 Iunto a la plaçuela,
Porque Barbolilla
Salga acà i nos vea;
Barbola, la hija
De la panadera,
75 La que suele darme
Tortas con manteca,
Porque algunas veces
Hacemos io i ella
Las vellaquerias
80 Detras de la puerta.

(CHACÓN: FOULCHÉ-DELBOSC, I, 8-10)[22]

Hermano Perico
que estás a la puerta
con camisa limpia
y montera nueva,
5 sayo alagartado,
jubón de las fiestas,
çapatos de dura,
de lazos y orejas,
calças atacadas
10 de gamuça y medias,
de color de Vayo
con sus rodilleras;
mi hermano Bartolo

[22] My translation of «Hermana Marica» follows: Sister Mary, you will not go to your school tomorrow, which is a holiday, nor will I go to mine. You will put on your bodice and your good dress skirt, embroidered collar, kerchief, and hair net. They will dress me in my new chemise, loose blue woolen coat, stockings of serge, and if it is good weather, I will bring my cloth cap that my grandmother gave me on Easter and, with its fringes, the red ribbon for my neck, which my neighbor brought me when he went to the fair. We will go to mass. We will see the church. My aunt the pot maker will give us a copper coin. We will buy with it (may no one find out) sweetmeats and chick-peas for the afternoon snack; and toward evening, in our small square, I will play at bullfighting, and you will play dolls with your two sisters, Juana and Magdalena, and your two little cousins, Mary and the one-eyed girl. And if mother wants to strike the castanets, you will be able to dance in the doorway, and to the sound of the tambourine, little Andrea will sing: «Your herbs, mother, did not do me any good.» And, out of paper, I will make a dress uniform dyed with mulberries, so that it will look good, and a peaked hood with many points. I will put as the cap's crown the two black feathers from the tail of the rooster that we killed with oranges there in the orchard three carnival days before Ash Wednesday. And on the long walking stick, I will put a banner with two white tassels on its fringe, and on my little cane hobby-horse, I will put a head of embossed leather, two threads for reins. And I and more than thirty others from the neighborhood will go bounding into the street. We will joust with reed spears near the small square so little Barbola will come out here and see us — Barbola, the daughter of the baker's wife, who usually gives me round cakes with butter, because sometimes she and I do mischievous tricks behind the door.

se va a Ingalaterra
15 a matar al Draque
y a prender la Reina
y a los Luteranos
de la Bandomesa.
Tiene de traerme
20 a mí de la guerra
un Luteranico
con una cadena,
y una Luterana
a señora agüela.
25 Vámonos yo y tú
para la açotea,
desde allí veremos
a las lexas tierras,
los montes y valles,
30 los campos y sierras;
mas si allá nos vamos,
diré una conseja
de la blanca niña
que tomó la Griega.
35 Yo tengo una poca
de miel y manteca,
turrón de Alicante
y una piña nueva:
haremos de todo
40 cochaboda y buena;
vamos, Dorotea,
a pasar la siesta,
y allá jugaremos
donde no nos vean.
45 Harás tú la niña
y yo la maestra,
veré tu dechado,
labor y tarea;
haré lo que suele
50 hazer la maestra
con la mala niña
que su labor yerra.
Tengo yo un cochito
con sus cuatro ruedas,
55 en que, Dorotea,
lleves tus muñecas;
un peso de limas,
hecho de dos medias,
y un correverás
60 que compré en la feria.
Cuando yo sea grande,
señora Dorotea,
tendré un caballito,
daré mil carreras,
65 tú saldrás a verme

por entre las rejas,
casarme he contigo,
habrá boda y fiesta,
dormiremos juntos
70   en cama de seda,
y haremos un niño
que vaya a la escuela.

(GONZÁLEZ PALENCIA, I, 61-62)

Although «Hermano Perico» is anonymous, some critics, such as Juan Millé and Ángel González Palencia, believe that Góngora wrote it. Others, such as Emilio Carilla, however, doubt that Góngora is the author.[23] The major feature distinguishing «Hermano Perico» from «Hermana Marica» is the tone of each text's final lines. Whereas the last four verses of «Hermana Marica» astonish and amuse the reader who is expecting a more delicate conclusion to the poem, the twelve final verses of «Hermano Perico» eliminate any chance of a surprise ending. The first eight prepare the reader for a change of tone, and the last four dissipate the poem's humorous conclusion. The point of the final verses of «Hermano Perico» is life's cyclical nature. The protagonist is dreaming about the future in which he will grow up and marry Dorothea. The love he seeks is lustful but legitimized by marriage; and the outcome of it will be the creation of a second Perico who will go to the same school and enjoy the same childish pleasures as his father.

Seven years after the completion of «Hermana Marica», Góngora wrote «Hanme dicho, hermanas» in which, as a young adult, he shocks the *beatas* of his time as he flippantly addresses a group of nuns to whom he mockingly describes himself. More closely related to «Hermana Marica», however, is the anonymous poem «Hermana Juanilla»; its initial lines are particularly suggestive of a Góngora origin:

—«Hermana Juanilla,
entremos en cuenta,
dime, quién te dió
esa saya nueva?
5   Que si ayer andabas
la [*sic*] carnes de fuera,
en tan poco espacio
no se adquieren prendas.
Tu no juegas dados,
10   parar, ni carteta,
para que digamos
que ganaste hacienda.
Tienes gargantillas,

---

[23] MILLÉ, *Sobre la génesis*, pp. 94-95. GONZÁLEZ PALENCIA, «Indice de primeros versos», II, 381: «'Hermano Perico', 82 (Góngora?).» See also CARILLA, p. 36.

cintas y agujetas,
15 guantes de polvillo,
valón, y arandela.
Dí, ¿quién de fregona
te hizo callejera?,
¿quién te puso en toldo?,
20 ¿quién te dió chinelas?
Las de toldo y rumbo
en aquestas ferias,
no ganarán mucho,
si hay tantas rameras.
25 Abarata el pan,
si hay mucho en la tierra,
y en lo mas barato,
la gente se ceba.
Digo que estás linda,
30 mas recelo aun huelas
al sucio estropajo
con que siempre fregas.
Tu toca, Juanilla,
tus sortijas puestas,
35 tú te pones blanco,
con color te afeitas.
Pues a fé que tienes
si anda bien la cuenta
encima de ti,
40 una cuarentena.
No sé que te han visto,
que no eres Lucrecia,
mas eres Medusa,
o astuta Medea.
45 Maldito sea el gusto
que a ti se sujeta,
mas al fin en gustos,
hay mil diferencias.
Baxa un poco el toldo,
50 gravedad a fuera,
que para conmigo
serás la que eras.
A quien no conoce
tus infames prendas,
55 te haz Penelope,
o casta Minerva.
Déxame de cuentos,
afable te muestra,
que el mudar de estado
60 no es razón te vuelva.
Nunca estás en casa,
mis calles paseas,
poniendote, Juana,
casi en almoneda.
65 Mas pues no respondes

a tantas arengas,
doite por culpada,
que quien calla acepta.»
(González Palencia, II, 12-13)

«Hermana Marica» is more similar to «Hermano Perico» than to «Hermana Juanilla», but the two anonymous poems show a Góngora influence. One or both of them may be by Góngora. However, the authorship of either «Hermano Perico» or «Hermana Juanilla» is indeterminable because not enough is known about the history of these poems. Whereas the variant texts of «Grandes mas que elephantes i que habadas» closely resemble each other and, like the different versions of «Trepan los Gitanos», are chronologically related, there is no clear link between «Hermana Marica», «Hermano Perico», and «Hermana Juanilla». The three *romancillos* discussed here and the two versions of «Los raios le quenta al Sol» are complex examples of the textual problems plaguing much of Góngora's verse and of Spanish Golden Age poetry.

A SELECTED LIST OF WORKS CONSULTED

Aguirre, José Luis: *Góngora, su tiempo y su obra; estudio crítico sobre Polifemo* (Madrid: MAS, 1960).

Alemany y Selfá, Bernardo: *Vocabulario de las obras de don Luis de Góngora y Argote* (Madrid: RAE, 1930).

Alonso, Dámaso: *Góngora y el «Polifemo».* 5th ed., 3 vols. (Madrid: Gredos, 1967).

— «Puño y letra de don Luis en un manuscrito de sus poesías». In his *Estudios y ensayos gongorinos* (Madrid: Gredos, 1955), pp. 251-62.

Alonso, Dámaso and Eulalia Galvarriato de Alonso, eds.: *Para la biografía de Góngora: documentos desconocidos* (Madrid: Gredos, 1962).

Ares Montes, José: *Góngora y la poesía portuguesa del siglo XVII* (Madrid: Gredos, 1956).

Artigas, Miguel: *Don Luis de Góngora y Argote* (Madrid: RAE, 1925).

— *Semblanza de Góngora* (Madrid: Blass, 1928).

Askins, Arthur Lee-Francis, ed.: *Cancioneiro de corte e de magnates.* University of California Publications in Modern Philology, No. 84 (Berkeley: University of California Press, 1968).

Bates, Margaret J.: *«Discreción» in the Works of Cervantes* (Washington, D.C.: The Catholic University of America Press, 1945).

Besses, Luis: *Diccionario de argot español o lenguaje jergal gitano, delincuente profesional y popular* (Barcelona: Sucesores de Manuel Soler, 1906).

Cabrera de Córdoba, Luis: *Relaciones de las cosas sucedidas en la Corte de España desde 1599 hasta 1614* (Madrid: J. M. Alegría, 1857).

Camões, Luiz de: *Obras completas.* 7 vols. (Porto: Imprensa Portugueza, 1873).

— *Rimas.* 3 vols. (Lisboa: Na Officina de Antonio Craesbeeck de Mello, 1666-69).

Cañes, Francisco: *Diccionario español-latino-arábigo.* 3 vols. (Madrid: A. Sancha, 1787).

Carballo Picazo, Alfredo: «El soneto 'Mientras por competir con tu cabello', de Góngora». *RFE,* 47 (1964), 379-98.

Carilla, Emilio: «Notas gongorinas». *RFE,* 45 (1962), 32.

Cervantes Saavedra, Miguel de: *El ingenioso hidalgo Don Quijote de la Mancha.* Ed. Juan Antonio Pellicer. 2 vols. (Madrid: Gabriel de Sancha, 1797-98).

Chen, Juan de, ed.: *Laberinto amoroso* (Barcelona: Sebastián de Cormellas, 1618). Vignette ed. Karl Vollmöller. *RF,* 6 (1891), 89-138.

Churton, Edward: *Góngora.* 2 vols. (London: John Murray, 1862).

Córdoba, Fray Juan de: *Arte en lengua zapoteca* (Mexico: Pedro Balli, 1578).

Corominas, Joan: *Diccionario crítico etimológico de la lengua castellana.* 4 vols. Vols. I-II (Madrid: Gredos, 1954). Vols. III-IV (Berna: Francke, 1954).

Cossío, José M.: «Candores, esplendores». *RO,* 4, No. 40 (1926), 110-14.

— «De bibliografía gongorina». *RFE,* 19 (1932), 64-65.

— *Romances de Góngora* (Madrid: RO, 1927).

Covarrubias Horozco, Sebastián de: *Tesoro de la lengua castellana o española* (Ma-

drid: Luis Sánchez, 1611). Facs. with the additions of Benito Remigio Noydens, which were published in the 1674 edition. Ed. Martín de Riquer (Barcelona: Horta, 1943).

CRAWFORD, J. P. WICKERSHAM: «Italian Sources of Góngora's Poetry». *RR*, 20 (1929), 122-30.

CUDDON, J. A.: *A Dictionary of Literary Terms* (New York City: Doubleday, 1977).

DEFOURNEAUX, MARCELIN: *Daily Life in Spain in the Golden Age*. Trans. Newton Branch (New York: Praeger, 1971).

DELEITO Y PIÑUELA, JOSÉ: *Sólo Madrid es corte* (Madrid: Espasa-Calpe, 1942).

Diccionario de la lengua castellana. 6 vols. (Madrid: RAE, 1726-39). Facs. *Diccionario de Autoridades*. 3 vols. (Madrid: Gredos, 1963).

Diccionario histórico de la lengua española. Vols. I-II (Madrid: RAE, 1933-36).

DURÁN, AGUSTÍN: *Cancionero y romancero* (Madrid: E. Aguado, 1829).

EGUILAZ Y YANGUAS, LEOPOLDO DE: *Glosario etimológico de las palabras españolas de origen oriental*, Granada, 1886; rpt. (Madrid: Atlas, 1974).

ENTRAMBASAGUAS, JOAQUÍN DE: *Estudios y ensayos sobre Góngora y el barroco* (Madrid: Nacional, 1975).

— *Góngora en Madrid* (Madrid: IEM, 1961).

ESPINOSA, PEDRO, comp.: *Primera parte de las flores de poetas ilustres de España* (Valladolid: Luis Sánchez, 1605). 2nd ed. Ed. Juan Quirós de los Ríos and Francisco Rodríguez Marín (Sevilla: E. Rasco, 1896).

FANSHAWE, Sir RICHARD: *Shorter Poems and Translations*. Ed. N. W. Bawcutt (Liverpool: Liverpool University Press, 1964).

FOULCHÉ-DELBOSC, RAYMOND: «Bibliographie de Góngora». *RHi*, 18 (1908), 73-161.

— «Romancero de la Biblioteca Brancacciana». *RHi*, 65 (1925), 345-96.

FRÍAS, DAMASIO DE: «Diálogo de la discreción». In *Diálogos de diferentes materias inéditos hasta ahora* (Madrid: G. Hernández and Galo Sáez, 1929), pp. 3-210.

FUCILLA, JOSEPH G.: «A Decade of Notes on Spanish Poetry». *SP*, 32 (1935), 40-54.

— «Góngora». In *Estudios sobre el petrarquismo en España. RFE*, Anejo No. 72 (Madrid: CSIC, 1960), pp. 252-57.

GARCÍA LORCA, FRANCISCO: «Análisis de un *romance* de Góngora». *RR*, 47 (1956), 13-26.

GÓNGORA Y ARGOTE, LUIS DE: *Letrillas*. Ed. Robert Jammes (Paris: Ediciones Hispano-Americanas, 1963).

— *Obras completas*. Ed. Juan Millé y Giménez and Isabel Millé y Giménez (Madrid: Aguilar, 1943).

— *Obras en verso del Homero español*. Ed. Juan López de Vicuña (Madrid: Imprenta del Reino, 1627). Facs. Ed. Dámaso Alonso. Clásicos Hispánicos, No. 1 (Madrid: CSIC, 1963).

— *Obras poéticas*. Ed. Raymond Foulché-Delbosc. 3 vols. 1921; rpt. (New York: HSA, 1970).

— *Segundo tomo de las obras*. Ed. Diego García de Salcedo Coronel (Madrid: Imprenta Real, 1644).

— *Sonetos*. Ed. Biruté Ciplijauskaité (Madison: HSMS, 1981).

— *Sonetos completos*. Ed. Biruté Ciplijauskaité (Madrid: Castalia, 1969).

— *Todas las obras de don Luis de Góngora en varios poemas*. Ed. Gonzalo de Hoces y Córdoba (Madrid: Imprenta Real, 1633).

GONZÁLEZ PALENCIA, ANGEL, ed.: *Romancero general 1600, 1604, 1605*. Clásicos Españoles, III-IV, 2 vols. (Madrid: CSIC, 1947).

GUILLÉN, JORGE: *Language and Poetry* (Cambridge, MA: Harvard University Press, 1961).

HAGSTRUM, JEAN: *The Sister Arts* (Chicago: University of Chicago Press, 1958).

HENEL, HEINRICH: «Metaphor and Meaning». In *The Disciplines of Criticism*. Ed. Peter Demetz, Thomas Greene, and Lowry Nelson (New Haven: Yale University Press, 1968), pp. 93-123.

HESPELT, HERMAN E.: «A Variant of One of Góngora's Ballads». *MLN*, 45 (1930), 160-61.

JAMMES, ROBERT: *Études sur l'oeuvre poétique de Don Luis de Góngora y Argote* (Bordeaux: IEIIAUB, 1967).

KOMANECKY, PETER M.: «The 'Primera soledad' of Don Luis de Góngora y Argote: An Edition with Commentary». Unpubl. Ph.D. diss. The Johns Hopkins University, 1972.

LANSON, GUSTAVE: «Études sur les rapports de la littérature française et de la littérature espagnole au XVIIᵉ siècle (1600-1660)». *RHL*, 3 (1896), 321-31.

LAPESA, RAFAEL: «Sobre algunos sonetos de Garcilaso». In *La poesía de Garcilaso*. Ed. Elias L. Rivers (Barcelona: Ariel, 1974).

LEÓN, VÍCTOR: *Diccionario de argot español y lenguaje popular*. 2nd ed. (Madrid: Alianza, 1981).

LUGONES, LEOPOLDO: *Diccionario etimológico del castellano usual* (Buenos Aires: AAL, 1944).

MACHADO, JOSÉ P.: *Dicionário etimológico da língua portuguesa*. 2nd ed., 3 vols. (Lisboa: Confluência, 1967-73).

MADRIGAL, MIGUEL DE, comp.: *Segunda parte del Romancero general y flor de diversa poesía* (Valladolid: Antonio García, 1605). Ed. Joaquín de Entrambasaguas, 2 vols. (Madrid: CSIC, 1948).

MÉNDEZ PLANCARTE, ALFONSO: *Cuestiúnculas gongorinas* (Mexico: Andrea, 1955).

MENÉNDEZ PIDAL, RAMÓN: *Orígenes del español. RFE*, Anejo No. 1 (Madrid: Hernando, 1926).

— «Poesía popular y poesía tradicional en la literatura española». In *Los romances de América y otros estudios*, 6th ed. (Buenos Aires: Austral, 1958), pp. 52-87.

MENÉNDEZ Y PELAYO, MARCELINO: *Estudios de crítica histórica y literaria*. 7 vols. (Buenos Aires: Espasa-Calpe, 1944).

MILLÉ Y GIMÉNEZ, JUAN: *Sobre la génesis del Quijote* (Barcelona: Araluce, 1930).

ONG, WALTER J.: «A Dialectic of Aural and Objective Correlatives». In *Perspectives on Poetry*. Ed. James L. Calderwood and Harold E. Toliver (New York: Oxford University Press, 1968), pp. 119-31.

PABST, WALTER: *La creación gongorina en los poemas «Polifemo» y «Soledades»*. Trans. Nicolás Marín (Madrid: CSIC, 1966).

PAULSON, RONALD: *The Fictions of Satire* (Baltimore: The Johns Hopkins University Press, 1967).

PELLICER, JUAN ANTONIO: *Vida de Miguel de Cervantes Saavedra* (Madrid: Gabriel de Sancha, 1800).

PINHEIRO DA VEIGA, TOMÉ: «Relación del bautismo de Felipe IV». In the *Fastiginia o fastos geniales*. Trans. Narciso Alonso Cortés (Valladolid: Imprenta del Colegio de Santiago, 1916), pp. 1-41.

PLINIUS SECUNDUS, GAIUS: *Historia natural*. Trans. Jerónimo Gómez de Huerta, 2 vols. (Madrid: Luis Sánchez, 1624-29).

QUEVEDO, FRANCISCO DE: *Obra poética*. Ed. José M. Blecua, 4 vols. (Madrid: Castalia, 1969).

REYES, ALFONSO: *Cuestiones gongorinas* (Madrid: Espasa-Calpe, 1927).

— *Trazos de historia literaria*, 2nd ed. (Buenos Aires: Espasa-Calpe, 1951).

RIVADENEYRA, M., ed.: *Poetas líricos de los siglos XVI y XVII*. Vols. XXXII and XLII of the BAE. Vol. XXXII (Madrid: M. Rivadeneyra, 1854). Vol. XLII, 2nd ed. (Madrid: Sucesores de Rivadeneyra, 1875).

RODRÍGUEZ-MOÑINO, ANTONIO, ed.: *Construcción crítica y realidad histórica en la poesía española de los siglos XVI y XVII* (Madrid: Castalia, 1968).
— «El romance de Góngora 'Servía en Orán al Rey' (Textos y notas para su estudio)». In his *La transmisión de la poesía española en los siglos de oro*. Ed. Edward M. Wilson (Barcelona: Ariel, 1976), pp. 17-28.
— *Poesía y cancioneros (siglo XVI)* (Madrid: n.p., 1968).
SÁNCHEZ, LUIS, comp.: *Romancero general*, Madrid, 1600; facs. rpt. (New York: De Vinne Press, 1904).
SLOMAN, ALBERT E.: «The Two Versions of Góngora's 'Entre los sueltos caballos'». *RFE*, 44 (1961), 435-41.
SMITH, C. COLIN, ed.: *Spanish Ballads* (Oxford: Pergamon, 1964).
SPAULDING, ROBERT K.: *How Spanish Grew* (Berkeley: University of California Press, 1975).
SPITZER, LEO: *La enumeración caótica en la poesía moderna* (Buenos Aires: Instituto de Filología, 1945).
— «The Folkloristic Pre-stage of the Spanish *Romance* 'Count Arnaldos'». *HR*, 23 (1955), 173-87 and 24 (1956), 64-66.
TASSO, BERNARDO: *Rime di Bernardo Tasso* (Vinegia: Ioan. Ant. da Sabio, 1534).
TORNER, EDUARDO M.: *Lírica hispánica* (Madrid: Castalia, 1966).
TURBAYNE, COLIN MURRAY: *The Myth of Metaphor* (New Haven: Yale University Press, 1962).
VALDIVIESO, JOSEF DE: *Varias descripciones del tiempo, y de las estaciones del año* (Palma: Felipe Guasp, 1817).
VEGA, GARCILASO DE LA: *Obras con anotaciones de Fernando de Herrera* (Sevilla: Alonso de la Barrera, 1580). Facs. Ed. Antonio Gallego Morell (Madrid: CSIC, 1973).
VOSSLER, KARL: *Formas poéticas de los pueblos románicos* (Buenos Aires: Losada, 1960).
WALKER, ERNEST P., et al.: *Mammals of the World*. 3 vols. (Baltimore: The Johns Hopkins Press, 1964).
WARDROPPER, BRUCE W.: «La más bella niña». *SP*, 63 (1966), 661-76.
WARNKE, FRANK J.: *Versions of Baroque* (New Haven: Yale University Press, 1972).
WELLEK, RENÉ: «The Concept of the Baroque in Literary Scholarship». In *Concepts of Criticism*. Ed. Stephen G. Nichols, Jr. (New Haven: Yale University Press, 1963).